EFFECTIVE TEAMWORK

BEING AN EFFECTIVE TEAM MEMBER

Technological advances, global competition, environmental and legal issues...these and other forms of workplace turbulence mean that companies have to constantly adapt. One way companies have adapted is by using teams in the workplace. In fact, leaders in business and industry increasingly point to being able to work collaboratively as a key to success in a worldwide economic environment.

Working together is often called collaboration, which literally means "to labor together." Collaborating in the workplace has many benefits:

- Accomplish tasks any one individual can't. Many projects are too large or too complicated to complete alone.
- Brainstorm more effectively. Various people studying the same problem will find different solutions. A team can put together a solution that includes all or parts of the best individual ideas.
- Troubleshoot better. Many people analyzing a problem or a proposed solution can flush out all the pitfalls, making the final solution that much stronger.
- Build a community. Team members can form personal bonds. This is good for both the individuals and for workplace morale.

So, do you know the secret to being an effective team member? All you have to do is apply your multiple talents, skills, and energies toward achieving the team's purpose.

The goal of this course is to teach you how to do your part to ensure you make your team the best it can be.

In a high-performance team, you can feel the positive team environment. Such a team consistently meets its objectives.

And team members work together as one unit to solve problems.

In this course, you'll learn techniques to help you become even more effective and valued as you maximize your role as a team member. You'll explore ways to adopt a positive approach to being on a team as you develop and maintain a positive mindset about your team. You'll also learn how to be proactive and how to demonstrate tolerance toward team members. And you'll understand how to work collaboratively to achieve your team's goals.

ADOPT A POSITIVE ATTITUDE

Benefits of a positive team attitude
When you were first chosen to be a member of a team, were you excited? Or were you annoyed or even apprehensive? Did you enter this new phase of your professional life with enthusiasm and high hopes, or with mainly negative expectations?

Whether you realize it or not, your thoughts and feelings are reflected in your actions. When you're happy and satisfied, your teammates know it. And when you aren't – they know that too.

Just one team member's bad attitude can have negative effects on a team. An unhappy or upset team member can be annoying at best and, at worst, demotivating for the other members. Bad attitudes diminish team effectiveness, especially if other members disassociate from the negative person.

In contrast, having a positive attitude about the team experience has many benefits:

a positive attitude keeps team members from wasting the team's time with complaints, making the entire group more productive

thinking positively about having to work on a team makes the experience more enjoyable for everyone, and

team members who perceive feedback from other team members as a positive thing will be less defensive and will also be more likely to make changes that will result in improved team performance

See each benefit for an example of what a high-performance team member has to say about the benefits of having a positive outlook.

More productive
"Looking back, I can't believe the amount of time I wasted thinking negative thoughts. If I could have all that time back, I'd be years younger. By keeping my thoughts and attitude more positive, I've increased my productivity each day."

More enjoyable
"I had always been a loner; the move to teams really bugged me. Then I attended a positive-thinking seminar, and it helped me change my attitude toward teamwork. When my outlook changed, I began to experience more enjoyment from my team experience."

Improved team performance
"I used to get so frustrated having to get other people's input. It seemed to take forever to get anything done, and I felt constantly under attack. Then I realized it was my viewpoint that was
causing me frustration, and that input from my team members was helping us all do a better job."

Whether your mental mind-set needs a routine maintenance checkup or a major overhaul, it's up to you to perform the necessary work.
Then you'll be able to reap the benefits of adjusting your outlook on teams.

Question
What are the benefits of having a positive attitude about the team experience?
Options:
1. You can help keep from wasting time with complaints
2. You can have a more enjoyable team experience
3. You can help improve the team's overall performance
4. You can eliminate conflict with your teammates
5. You can ensure you meet your deadlines Answer

Option 1: *This is a correct option. Without a positive outlook, you* tend to focus on the frustration or the negative, which is a waste of time. When you focus on the positive, the whole group can be more productive.

Option 2: This is a correct option. Adjusting your outlook to have a positive attitude means you'll gain more enjoyment from the team experience, and so will your team members.

Option 3: This is a correct option. When you think of feedback from others on the team as a positive thing, you'll be less defensive and more likely to get greater results.

Option 4: This option is incorrect. Adjusting your outlook about working with a team does not mean an end to all conflict. However, a positive outlook will help you to handle the conflict better.

Option 5: This option is incorrect. Even having a positive outlook won't guarantee you'll always meet all your deadlines. It will help you handle deadline stress better, though.

Strategies for a positive team attitude

Do you believe – truly believe – that your participation on the team can benefit you and the team as a whole? Hopefully, you do, because your belief is critical to how you'll act on the team. Your actions will affect everyone on the team and the team's ability to achieve its purpose.

You can align your beliefs and your actions by implementing these strategies for developing and maintaining a positive mind-set about the team experience:

- Concentrate on the positive aspects of your team members. If a teammate gets under your skin, focus on his good traits.
- Focus on the benefits of working on a team. Understand that a group of like-minded professionals can always accomplish more than a single mind working alone.
- Accept and learn from mistakes and experiences, and then move on. Mistakes can teach you as much as successes, and your response to them can turn a negative into a positive.

As an example, consider the situation of a software development team. Lisa is a programmer, and one of her teammates, Fred, is being extremely picky about the details of the interface style for an application.

He's going over and over one point in a team meeting, and Lisa is getting aggravated. How can Lisa apply the strategy for concentrating on Fred's good qualities?

Question
What could Lisa say in the programmers' team meeting to show she's had an attitude change?

Options:
1. "Fred, what about functionality? We should decide what other things our application should do to make sure we choose the right database."
2. "Fred is bringing up a lot of details to consider. He obviously cares about achieving the highest possible quality. He wants it to be perfect, and rightly so. After all, what's the point in doing something if you aren't going to do it right?"
3. "Fred, while I appreciate your level of detail, we have to move on or we'll never get anything done."

Answer
Option 1: *This option is incorrect. Lisa may feel as though she's supporting Fred by being as picky as he is, but she won't change her attitude about him by using this technique.*
Option 2: *This is the correct option. Lisa is successfully using the strategy of finding Fred's*
good traits to change her own negative attitude to a positive mindset.
Option 3: *This option is incorrect. While Lisa is attempting to acknowledge one of Fred's good traits, she's really shutting him down at the same time.*

Lisa had such success with using the first strategy for adjusting her mind-set that she decides to try the second one as well.
She's currently a member of the design team for a new applica-

tion. Based on the results of today's team meeting, Lisa needs to rewrite a large chunk of code for the operating system.

Rather than focusing on the fact that she'll be working a lot of overtime in the next few weeks, she decides to concentrate on the benefits of working on a team. Lisa tells herself, "The team made great decisions today. The application wasn't as good as it could've been, but once I rewrite the code, it will be. Our customers are going to love its capabilities. If I wasn't working on a team, this software wouldn't be nearly as well thought out."

Human beings have a tendency to agonize over mistakes. Because of this, the last strategy in adopting a positive team attitude is a tough one for most people to apply.

Many people find it difficult to accept mistakes, learn from them, and then move on. The best way to approach this is to pull yourself up, rework any mistakes, and search for a better way.

When you make up your mind to be positive, you'll change the way you feel about yourself. This will help you learn from experience and overcome failure.

As an example, remember Fred, the excessively detailed computer programmer who worked with Lisa? In going back over his week, he realizes he was overly zealous and feels a little ashamed of himself.

But he makes a conscious decision to learn from it and move on. Fred says, "I tend to become too focused on details, and I need to address them with the team and then move on to other subjects. I know what to look out for so I don't make this mistake again."

You can apply this strategy to yourself, but you'll also need to remember it when confronted with other people's mistakes. Don't make other people feel bad when they make mistakes, either. After all, like you, they're only human.

Simply note any errors and what caused or led to them, and then learn from and work past them.

Question

What are the strategies for adopting a positive mind-set about working on a team?

Options:
1. Accepting mistakes and moving on
2. Focusing on the benefits of working on a team
3. Concentrating on the positive aspects of your team members
4. Concentrating on making all deadlines
5. Enhancing your career through being a good team member

Answer

Option 1: *This is a correct option. Accepting mistakes, learning from them, and moving on will help you proceed more effectively. This strategy will go a long way toward developing and maintaining a positive mind-set for the entire team.*

Option 2: *This is a correct option. This strategy helps you develop a positive mind-set through the realization that everyone working together can accomplish things more quickly than any one individual.*

Option 3: *This is a correct option. Focusing on the positive aspects of team members will help you empathize with them and focus on their good traits.*

Option 4: *This option is incorrect. Making deadlines is part of team activities, but it's not a strategy to adopt a positive mind-set.*

Option 5: *This option is incorrect. Enhancement of your career may be a benefit of being a good team player, but it's not a strategy to adopt a positive mind-set.*

Summary

There's no discounting the power and effect that having a good attitude can have on a team. The benefits of having a positive attitude can make a team more productive, can make the team more enjoyable for all members, and can lead to improved team performance.

Team members can adopt a positive mind-set about working on a team using a few simple strategies. They can accept mistakes, learn from them, and move on. They can focus on the benefits of working on a team. And they can concentrate on the positive aspects of team members.

BE PROACTIVE

Characteristics of proactive people
All great technological advancements – the light bulb, the airplane, and the personal computer – were created by innovators who imagined things that didn't yet exist. Being an outstanding team member requires a bit of an inventor's spirit. While it's easy to feel overwhelmed by deadlines and workload, a team needs to be proactive to achieve goals beyond the daily and weekly to-do lists.

When you're proactive, you anticipate occurrences and prepare for them in advance. But if you're reactive, you wait for things to happen, and then act in response. When it comes to teamwork, do you consider yourself proactive or reactive?

To help determine if your tendency is to be more proactive or reactive, choose the statement closest to what you might say.

I plan for the worst and hope for the best
This is a proactive philosophy. Being proactive encompasses a sense of being prepared for what might come. You consciously engineer your own events instead of merely reacting to things, so you can make your own future.

I take each day as it comes
Thinking along the lines that "life's too short to worry about tomorrow" is a reactive philosophy, which is how most people think. There are times when reacting to events is what's needed. But truly effective team members do more than instinctively react to stimuli.

Although proactive people take the initiative, it doesn't mean you have to be pushy, obnoxious, or aggressive. It does mean you need to acknowledge your responsibility to make things happen.

Being proactive helps you institute systems that make life easier – not just you, but for others as well. Proactive people are often regarded as instigators of action and creative ideas.

Being proactive is a great method for avoiding extra work or rework, since it helps you anticipate problems in advance. And that same trait is extremely important for averting real disasters, not just inconveniences.

Having a proactive attitude impacts you personally and makes a difference to your team as a whole. As a proactive person, you'll reap the following benefits:

- You'll have energy and enthusiasm. And the energy will be contagious, spreading throughout the team.
- You'll have good planning skills. When you're proactive, you look into the future to find out what you and your team will need to do.
- You'll have troubleshooting and problem-solving abilities. You'll always be searching for signs of potential problems and using creativity to solve them.
- You'll enhance your communication skills, because you'll be anticipating questions others may have. This allows you to be clear and thorough, transmitting the information your team needs.

Proactive teams are typically effective and energetic. The enthusiasm they generate feeds on itself, their output is creative, and they can anticipate problems. Proactive mind-sets help teams avoid crises.

Of course, sometimes, in spite of everyone's best efforts, problems arise that need immediate attention. A team also needs some reactive skills to manage an actual crisis situation.

But even in situations where immediate reactive action is needed, you can take a proactive approach to emergency events.

With careful planning, you can identify cues of an impending crisis and assign activities to avert it. This proactive approach is especially important to avoid unnecessary interventions and rework.

Appropriately reacting to an emergency situation and **being** reactive, though, are two separate things. Reactive team members often seem unorganized and irritated. They're usually focused on what is right in front of them and aren't prepared for anything new or unexpected. And they experience more stress, since they feel like they're always solving problems.

Question

What are the characteristics of a person who has a proactive attitude?

Options:

1. Is energetic, with contagious enthusiasm
2. Is a good planner
3. Is a good problem solver
4. Is a good communicator
5. Doesn't think beyond the issue at hand
6. Gets stressed when the unexpected happens

Answer

Option 1: *This is a correct option. Proactive people are energetic; their enthusiasm easily spreads throughout the team.*

Option 2: *This is a correct option. Proactive people are typically good planners, because they*
anticipate problems by forecasting what the team will need.

Option 3: *This is a correct option. Proactive people search for signs of potential problems and use creativity in analyzing those issues, which makes them good troubleshooters and problem solvers.*

Option 4: *This is a correct option. Proactive people are good communicators. They anticipate questions others may have, which allows them to be clear and thorough.*

Option 5: *This option is incorrect. A reactive attitude can be of benefit – such as during a crisis – when you focus entirely on the issue at hand. But having a proactive attitude will help you prepare for and prevent crises.*

Option 6: *This option is incorrect. Reactive people typically get* *stressed, since they aren't prepared for the unexpected.*

Being a proactive team member

What do you think – is it time you took a more proactive stance? If so, you aren't the only team member who's had to switch gears from being reactive to proactive. A lot of people have to make that same mental shift, but it helps take teams to a high level of performance.

But rest assured that you'll gain some important personal benefits by becoming a more proactive team member. You'll increase your effectiveness and contribution to the team. You'll feel more empowered to help the team meet its objectives. And you may be seen as having leadership abilities.

The basic principles of being proactive are simple but effective:

- identify opportunities for action by searching for potential problems, errors, and causes of concern, and
- get consent or acceptance from the rest of the team, which increases the chances that your proactive ideas will succeed

See each of the basic principles of being proactive for more information.

Identify opportunities for action

Too often a team makes decisions by being backed into a corner and having no other choices. The key to being proactive is to choose and do before you have to. To identify opportunities for action, look everywhere to find things that might be improved. As soon as you've clearly identified all problem areas, plan a course of action to address those areas.

Get consent from the rest of the team

Being proactive and having new ideas sometimes means dealing with fear, a lack of support, and resistance to change.

In an ideal teamwork situation, all teammates are asked for their input. Nobody is forced to abide by changes he didn't hear about first. If you want to make changes that will affect your team, talk them over and get a consensus first.

Lance is a team member on his company's computer help desk. He's constantly being asked questions, many of which are the same or cover the same areas of concern. Follow along as he takes a proactive approach to his work.

Lance identifies an opportunity for action when he thinks about how many times a day he and his teammates answer the same questions. He realizes that the company could really increase efficiency if employees had access to a list of frequently asked questions, or FAQs.

Lance brings up the idea in a team meeting, and gets immediate acceptance from the rest of the team. He immediately begins writing down FAQs that spring to mind. Then he circulates the list among all team members so they can add to it and make it more robust.

Lance gets other team members to sign off on the finished list after he has consensus on the questions to be included.

Lance used the basic principles of being proactive. Instead of just reacting to the same questions over and over in the course of his workday, he looked around and identified an opportunity. He realized that a list of FAQs would help his team and the company's employees who were calling for help. So he got consent from the rest of the team for the project and then included their input.

Lance also had the team members sign off on the finished product. This maximized the team's buy-in to the new tool.

Question

Which are examples of being a proactive team member?

Options:
1. An HR team member develops a checklist of what to include in a new-hire welcome packet
2. An editorial team member gets her team to sign off on using a more efficient fact-checking process
3. An engineering team member repairs a machine that isn't operating properly
4. A housekeeping team member in a hotel begins cleaning the room areas in a different order

Answer

Option 1: *This is a correct option. Identifying opportunities for action, such as a missing checklist, is a proactive strategy for the HR team member.*

Option 2: *This is a correct option. Getting consent from the rest of the team will help ensure the team's buy-in to the new process.*

Option 3: *This option is incorrect. Repairing a machine after it's broken down is a reactive strategy. A proactive strategy would include preventive maintenance to avoid the breakdown in the first place.*

Option 4: *This option is incorrect. Taking pre-emptive action by tackling a job in a different order is neither identifying an opportunity for action nor getting consent from the team.*

Summary

People with proactive attitudes are typically energetic, with plenty of enthusiasm. They're good planners, because part of being proactive is looking ahead to find out what will be needed. They're alert to signs of problems that might arise, and they're creative in coming up with ways to solve those problems. They're also good communicators, because they anticipate questions others might have.

Strategies to enhance your ability to be a proactive team member include identifying opportunities for action and getting consent or acceptance from other members of the team.

BE TOLERANT

Acknowledge the right to differ

How do you behave toward people who are different from you in day-to-day business? Do you argue with them? Point out what you perceive to be their errors? Do you smile slightly and ignore them, or do you listen to their viewpoints with an open mind?

When you're receptive to the diverse opinions, perceptions, and beliefs of others, you give yourself permission to grow and change – to become a better teammate.

As a team member, you can use two strategies to demonstrate tolerance on your team: acknowledge others' rights to hold differing opinions, and treat others with respect.

Team members who don't listen to what others have to say before expressing their viewpoints aren't acknowledging the right to have a different opinion. This is also true of members who interrupt, speak over, butt in, or cut off their teammates.

Imagine a situation where a teammate is the only person on one side of an argument, and he's standing his ground in defense of his idea. Instead of trying to explain why he's wrong, take a minute to remember how it felt when you were the person holding an unpopular opinion in the group. Then take a deep breath and wade back into the argument, but this time, instead of arguing for your side, offer a supportive statement on behalf of your lone teammate.

A supportive statement validates a person's right to hold a differing opinion. It doesn't mean you've suddenly decided he's right; it just means you're acknowledging his right to hold an opinion different from yours.

An excellent example of a supportive statement is "I don't necessarily agree with you, but I'm willing to listen to what you have to say."

Helping a team develop a shared understanding, while honoring members' differing viewpoints, is always important.

Diversity of cultural viewpoints can be particularly enriching for a team, though team members must make the effort to appreciate and understand the differences between them.

Meanings and interpretations can vary in different cultures. But cultural differences can be turned to advantage with openness and understanding.

Treat others with respect

Ask any of your coworkers how they want to be treated at work. No matter what their cultural background, they'll likely top their list with the desire to be treated with dignity and respect. To address this, you can use the second strategy in demonstrating tolerance by showing respect through simple yet powerful actions. This will help you avoid being unintentionally disrespectful, too.

When you demonstrate respect for others, you protect their self-esteem and build a relationship based on trust and cooperation.

Teams demonstrating respect have certain characteristics in common. Their members treat each other with courtesy, politeness, and kindness, and they encourage coworkers to express opinions and ideas.

Members also praise more frequently than they criticize. Such teams encourage praise and recognition from employee to employee, as well as from the supervisor.

Team members who insult, name call, disparage, or put down people or their ideas are most definitely not treating others with respect. This is also true of members who nitpick, criticize little things, belittle, judge, demean, or patronize.

Keep in mind that a series of seemingly trivial actions, added up over time, can constitute bullying, which is one of the worst forms of disrespect.

Several strategies exist to help you demonstrate that you treat others with respect:

Use objective language instead of critical or judgmental language. Objective language focuses on the issue, not on the person.

Limit the use of "you" when you must point out problems. Say "I" and "we" instead. "You" statements come across as judgmental and controlling; "I" and "we" statements focus people on the issue, not the placement of blame or judgment.

Whenever possible, add provisional qualifiers to your statements. Provisional qualifiers suggest that the speaker understands he's about to deliver an opinion, not place blame, and that he's open to other points of view.

See each strategy for examples of the kind of wording that demonstrates respect.

Use nonjudgmental, objective language

A team member using objective language might say "We've completed 80% of our goal this month." A critical or judgmental phrasing would be "You're behind schedule."

Use "I" and "we" statements

A team member limiting the use of "you" might say "We need to get a better handle on the problem." The same issue stated in a judgmental way would be "You don't understand the problem."

Use provisional qualifiers

Examples of provisional qualifiers include, "In my opinion," "I may be wrong," "It seems to me," "It's been my experience," and "According to the data I've researched."

Remember to demonstrate tolerance and respect to all people, no matter their race, religion, gender, country of origin, or any other protected status. Team policies and procedures should be implemented consistently so people feel that they're treated fairly and equally.

Question

EFFECTIVE TEAMWORK

Based on what you've just learned, match strategies for showing tolerance of teammates with their corresponding examples.

Options:
A. Demonstrate respect by using "I" or "we"
B. Acknowledge the right to hold a differing opinion
C. Demonstrate respect by using objective language
D. Demonstrate respect by using provisional qualifiers

Targets:
1. "We should re-examine the data to find the problem."
2. "I'm not sure I agree, but I'm willing to hear you out."
3. "Your opinion appears to be based on the available data."
4. "It's been my experience that data can be manipulated."

Answer

When using a statement such as "We should re-examine the data to find the problem," you're demonstrating respect by using the pronoun "we" instead of "you."

When you state you don't agree, but are willing to listen, you acknowledge the right to hold a differing opinion. This doesn't necessarily mean you're agreeing with the other person, only that it's OK for the person to have her own opinion.

You can demonstrate respect by using objective language, rather than critical language. An example is saying that someone's opinion appears to be based on the available data, showing you have understood the information.

An example of demonstrating respect is using provisional qualifiers. Using phrases like "It's been my experience" shows you're sharing an opinion, rather than placing blame.

Follow along as team members Keith, Elaine, and Adam interact with one another in a purchasing meeting. Notice how the team member with the differing opinion is treated.

Keith: I think we should interview several vendors before making a decision.

Elaine: Why waste our time? We've been using the same vendor for years; everyone loves him and his products.

Adam: Let's hear what Keith has to say, Elaine.

Keith: Thanks. I know the team has been using the same vendor, and I'm not suggesting we get rid of him. I am suggesting we talk to his competitors to find out whether his rates are still competitive and his products are on target for our current needs.

Elaine: You're just trying to stir up trouble.

Adam: It seems to me Keith's idea has merit. If nothing else, our current vendor might cut us a new deal if he thinks we might take our business elsewhere.

Which team member do you think demonstrated tolerance of Keith's opinion? Did either of his teammates give Keith a chance to state his point of view? Did either of his teammates make a supportive statement to make it clear he or she was willing to listen to Keith? These questions help you evaluate how well Elaine and Adam applied the strategies for demonstrating tolerance on a team. But you can use the questions to evaluate your own team as well.

Question

Which team member do you think demonstrated tolerance of Keith's opinion by acknowledging a teammate's right to hold a differing opinion?

Options:

1. Adam 2. Elaine

Answer

Option 1: *This is the correct option. Adam said, "Let's hear what Keith has to say, Elaine," which showed that Adam was acknowledging Keith's right to his opinion.*

Option 2: *This option is incorrect. When Keith's opinion was to interview several vendors before making a decision, Elaine shut him down by saying "Why waste our time?" This doesn't demonstrate tolerance.*

When evaluating if either of Keith's teammates treated the other team members with respect, consider the following questions. Did they use the pronouns "I" or "we" instead of "you"? Did either use objective language instead of judgmental language, and did they use provisional qualifiers?

Question
Which team member do you think demonstrated tolerance of Keith's opinion by using the strategy of treating others with respect?
Options:
1. Adam
2. Elaine

Answer
Option 1: *This is the correct option. Adam used a provisional qualifier when he said "It seems to me Keith's idea has merit." This statement of Adam's also validated Keith's right to his opinion.*
Option 2: *This option is incorrect. Elaine said "You're just trying to stir up trouble," which is not objective and uses "you" instead of the pronouns "I" or "we." This statement doesn't demonstrate tolerance or respect for Keith and his ideas.*

As you just learned from your evaluation of the scenario, Elaine didn't want to hear anything Keith said because his opinion was different from hers. She didn't even attempt to apply either of the strategies for demonstrating tolerance.
Adam, however, applied both strategies. First, he validated Keith's right to state his opinion. Then, he treated Keith with respect by using a provisional qualifier and conceding Keith's point.
If you had a choice to act like Elaine or Adam – and you do, by the way – which type of behavior would you choose? Most likely you'd choose Adam's way, because he applied the strategies successfully. And in doing so, he treated Keith the way you would probably want to be treated.

Question
Wayne was recently transferred to a new sales department. Although he has years of sales experience, one of his coworkers, Joan, thinks he's inexperienced. In a recent team meeting, Joan brought up a problem with a particularly picky customer who

demands a lot of information, and Wayne made a suggestion to tell the customer everything.

Which are examples of what Joan could say to demonstrate tolerance?

Options:
1. "In my experience, very few clients want input that isn't sugarcoated."
2. "I'm not sure I understand where this is going, Wayne, but go ahead."
3. "Well, we have tried that approach with other clients, and we didn't have much luck."
4. "Wayne, you've only been here for one week. How can you have a story to tell already?"
5. "I don't think you understand the background of the situation."

Answer

Option 1: *This option is correct. Joan is demonstrating respect by using the provisional qualifier "In my experience."*

Option 2: *This option is correct. Joan is acknowledging Wayne's right to hold a differing opinion by encouraging him to express it.*

Option 3: *This option is correct. Joan is demonstrating respect by using the "we" pronoun, instead of using judgmental phrasing and "you" statements directed at Wayne.*

Option 4: *This is an incorrect option. Joan is using critical and nonobjective language, as well as "you" statements. This neither acknowledges that Wayne has a right to his own opinion, nor does it demonstrate respect for him.*

Option 5: *This is an incorrect option. While this statement begins with an "I," Joan is really being rather condescending toward Wayne, showing little tolerance.*

Summary

Whether you're dealing with a coworker or a stranger, being tolerant is important in creating happy and high-performing teams. When it comes to teamwork, a climate of trust, respect, and cooperation allows you to share ideas freely and leads to more robust decision making.

Strategies for demonstrating tolerance of teammates include acknowledging the right for others to hold differing opinions and treating others with respect. When people are treated respectfully, they generally treat others in the same fashion. You can demonstrate respect by using nonjudgmental, objective language, using "I" and "we" statements, and using provisional qualifiers in your speech.

COLLABORATE WITH OTHERS

Strategies for working collaboratively
In your nonworking life, have you ever met people who try to do everything themselves? Maybe you play on a sports team with a ball-hog, or perhaps you volunteer at a charity with someone who thinks only he can organize an event correctly. The same type of behavior can evidence on a work team when one team member tries to do all the work and inhibits others from participating. High-functioning teams need everyone to collaborate, not to compete.

If you were asked, would you be able to explain the difference between collaboration and cooperation?

When a group of individuals work together in an agreeable manner, the members engage in cooperative teamwork.

But true collaborative teamwork involves individuals working together as a single unit. In such a case, each team member brings value and helps create a synergistic team environment.

High-performance teams, by definition, are teams that engage in collaborative teamwork. To help your team become a high-performance team, you'll need to apply the strategies for working collaboratively with teammates by sharing pertinent knowledge with the team and putting the team's needs ahead of your own.

When you share information with your team members, you build trust and decrease errors based on false assumptions or lack of information.

When you learn new information of possible importance to

your team, tell your teammates. Together you can find ways to use the information to better your product or service and benefit your team.

To determine whether you share information effectively, ask yourself a few questions. If you know something that you could – and should – share with your teammates, do you? Did you ever keep something back for your own use or pleasure? If you don't share information, will the team suffer for it?

Question

Be sure to share news in a professional manner. If you sound gossipy or teasing, you could irritate or alienate teammates. For example, imagine you've just learned that your company's main competitor is about to be purchased by another company.

Which way of sharing this information with your teammates would be most effective?

Options:

1. "Do I have some juicy news to tell you guys..."
2. "I've learned some sensitive information that could affect our team." 3. "I've learned something, but I can't tell you just yet."

Answer

Option 1: *This is an incorrect option. You're obviously willing to share your information, which is good, but you're heralding the news in a gossipy way. It's more effective to introduce your news in a professional manner.*

Option 2: *This is the correct option. In a professional manner, you're introducing the fact you know something, and you're alerting your teammates to the sensitivity of the issue.*

Option 3: *This is an incorrect option. If you're sworn to secrecy, don't hint around. Doing so could cause your teammates to mistrust you. And if you do know something that could affect your team, and you're free to tell it, then do so in a professional manner.*

The second strategy for working collaboratively is to put the needs of the team first. Sometimes team members have to perform tasks they don't want to, and one of the hardest things for people to do is sacrifice their individuality or personal desires. But if you want your team to be a high-performance team, you have to do what's best for it – not you.

Question

What would you say if your manager told you she wanted you to go on a business trip with a team member whose professional abilities you respect, but who – on a personal level – you just can't stand?

Which response do you think would be the most effective?

Options:

1. "I want the team to succeed, and this is a small sacrifice."
2. "My mantra will be 'it's only temporary.'"
3. "While I can work with her, I won't travel with her."

Answer

Option 1: This is the correct option. This is the best response because you're letting your boss know that going out of town with this teammate isn't your number one choice, but that the results will be worth it. You're putting the team's needs ahead of your own.

Option 2: This is an incorrect option. While you have a right to let your boss know you aren't thrilled, this isn't the best response. Even though you're putting the team's needs ahead of your own, you're doing so reluctantly, and it doesn't sound as if you want to.

Option 3: This is an incorrect option. By refusing to go, you're definitely not putting the team's needs ahead of your own desires.

To truly apply the collaborative strategy of putting your team's needs first, you have to accept tasks with grace. Agree that you'll put the team ahead of your own priorities, and follow through. But if it starts to feel like you're being taken advantage of, then talk to the team lead or manager about it.

Individual ambition in the team environment can sometimes hurt the team, but it can also sometimes help. Whether a member's personal goals are to spend more time with his family or to enhance his career, teams need to acknowledge them so they don't prevent the team from reaching its goals. When you know what your teammates want to achieve, what you want to achieve, and what the team as a whole wants, it creates a bond between team members.

Question

You and Sally are teammates. Sally tells you that the team is going to miss tomorrow morning's deadline because she has fallen behind. Later that day, the team leader tells you the deadline has been pushed out to the end of the week.

Which examples demonstrate the strategies for working collaboratively with others?

Options:

1. You tell Sally "I have some spare time this afternoon. I'll help you get your work done."
2. You say "I had hoped we'd make the deadline, but I understand. Things
happen."
3. You tell Sally the news about the rescheduled deadline immediately.
4. You wait to tell Sally the news in hopes she can catch up and meet the new deadline.

Answer

Option 1: *This choice is correct. You're demonstrating you're a team and equally responsible for completing the work. This is an example of putting the team's needs ahead of your own.*

Option 2: *This choice is incorrect. You're not working collaboratively to find a solution to complete the work. You also haven't shared the information you've learned about the change in deadline.*

Option 3: *This is a correct option. The best approach is for you to be honest with Sally and tell her immediately. This will build trust.*

Option 4: *This is an incorrect option. If you want to build an honest relationship with teammates, you need to make sure they have the same information as you.*

Using strategies to maximize your role

You'll now be able to review all the strategies to help you

maximize your role on a team. The four strategy areas cover developing and maintaining a positive mind-set about the team, being proactive, demonstrating tolerance, and working collaboratively. Then you'll be presented with the strategies pulled together into one example.
After that, you'll have an opportunity to practice the strategies in a roleplay situation.

Marie is a member of a newly created Green Team in charge of the implementation of a sustainability initiative. It's going to be a tough sell at her traditional company, and she knows she's going to need a strong team that works well together. Her team includes Jenny, the team lead, and John, a team member whose aggressive attitude has always bothered Marie. She wants to be better able to work with John before the next team meeting.

Question
What could Marie do to get past her unhappiness with John's style and maximize her role on the Green Team?
Options:
1. Keep in mind that John was chosen for the team because of his strong background in recycling technologies
2. Keep in mind that while she doesn't like John, Jenny, the team lead, does
3. Realize that John's strong drive can be channeled to really push the initiative forward more quickly
4. Accept that he's just that way, and try not to work directly with him

Answer
Option 1: *This is a correct option. Marie can develop and maintain a positive mind-set about working on a team by concentrating on team members' positive aspects.*
Option 2: *This is an incorrect option. Marie isn't trying to find John's positive aspects by just reflecting on the fact that Jenny likes him.*
Option 3: *This is a correct option. Marie can develop and maintain a*

positive mind-set about working on a team by focusing on the benefits, such as by realizing that working together can help accomplish things faster.

Option 4: *This is an incorrect option. Marie should try to find John's positive aspects and learn to collaborate with him. This will help her develop and maintain a positive mind-set about working on a team.*

When Marie concentrates on John's positive aspects – such as the fact that his somewhat aggressive nature also gives him great drive and focus – she can improve her own mind-set about being on the team.

Now she's ready to find out if that translates into a more productive, and less divisive, team meeting.

Marie, John, and Jenny are waiting for their other teammates to arrive. Follow along as Marie tries to put her new attitude about John into action.

John: I know you don't like me, Marie, but it's just because I had a better idea about the new project.

John is belligerent.

Marie: I do sometimes feel intimidated by your level of drive and focus, but I appreciate your idea even though I don't agree that it's better.

Marie is careful.

John: It is so better! *John is belligerent.*

Marie: It seems to me we'll have to agree to disagree on the project ideas.

Marie is thoughtful.

Jenny: You know, one of things I was going to bring up today was scheduling monthly team-building exercises. I'd like the whole team to agree to it, including you two.

Jenny is neutral.

Marie: I think that's a great idea, and I'd like to be paired with John for the first one.

Marie is upbeat.

John: You would? Well, who knows? Maybe we can end up liking each other after all!

John is thoughtful.

Marie's strategies are working. She acknowledges her team member's right to have a different opinion using nonjudgmental, objective language and "I" statements. And she uses the provisional qualifier "It seems to me" and also uses a "we" statement. Marie is clearly demonstrating tolerance. And Jenny builds on that by being proactive. She identifies an opportunity for action with her idea about team-building exercises, and she gets consent from both John and Marie.

Question

Feeling good about how things are going with her team, Jenny is about to leave work early to go away for a long weekend. Her manager calls and tells her the green initiative the team is working on has been fast-tracked for this fiscal year instead of the next.

What should she do?

Options:

1. Tell the team immediately
2. Tell the team at the next team meeting
3. Wait until the team is discouraged and needs a boost before telling them

Answer

Option 1: *This is the correct option. Working collaboratively involves sharing all pertinent knowledge with the team as soon as it's available. In this case, that may involve putting the team's needs ahead of Jenny's own.*

Option 2: *This is an incorrect option. Jenny should share information with her team as soon as she gets it.*

Option 3: *This is an incorrect option. While the sentiment of wanting to boost her teammates' spirits is a nice one, Jenny will build trust and enhance collaboration by sharing information right away.*

Jenny successfully worked collaboratively by sharing the relevant information with her team, even though it required her to put the team's needs ahead of her own.

Now you'll have the chance to practice the strategies for maximizing your team effectiveness.

Dealing with mistakes is never easy. But taking the approaches of developing and maintaining a positive mind-set, being proactive, demonstrating tolerance, and working collaboratively will help maximize your role on a team.

Remaining nonjudgmental and using objective language demonstrate that team problems need team solutions. And by identifying opportunities for action and putting team needs ahead of your own, you can get past problems in a proactive and collaborative fashion.

Summary

To successfully maximize your role on a team, you need to practice strategies in four areas. The strategies for developing and maintaining a positive mind-set about the team are to concentrate on team members' positive aspects, focus on benefits of working on a team, and accept mistakes, learn from them, then move on. The techniques for being proactive include identifying opportunities for action and getting consent or acceptance from the rest of the team.

The strategies for demonstrating tolerance are to acknowledge others' rights to hold differing opinions; use nonjudgmental, objective language; use "I" and "we" statements; and use provisional qualifiers. And finally, the strategies for working collaboratively are to share pertinent knowledge with the team and to put the team's needs ahead of your own.

ESTABLISHING TEAM GOALS AND RESPONSIBILITIES

Any group of individuals will contain people with distinct personalities, specialized skills, and ideas of what they want to accomplish. So, just what makes a team, a team?

The one characteristic that distinguishes a team from an ordinary group of people is that the highest priority of its members is the accomplishment of team goals.

People on teams know that although each of them is a unique individual with special strengths and talents, the team won't go anywhere unless everyone is working together toward the same goal.

Working on a team has many benefits:

sharing the workload

evening out the highs and lows, and ebbs and flows to focus organizational energy on a shared goal

being able to discuss and resolve opportunities and constraints, and

tapping into diverse talents, knowledge, and experience

Setting goals and working toward them is crucial to the success of any team. But it's important that the team is prepared to achieve those goals.

Preparing your team for a project or initiative involves three basic steps. See each step for more information.

1. Establish team goals

To start, establish the team mission and goals for each individual team member. Goals are defined through a collective effort by asking the right questions and constructing specific, measurable objectives. Goals also need to be clear and measurable, and linked to overall corporate goals.

2. Allocate responsibilities

The second step is to assign the goals to team members based on their strengths and experience. Allocating responsibilities involves aligning team roles and team members' competencies. At this point, you'll identify the roles on your team, assess team members' competencies, and assign or accept responsibilities.

3. Clarify expectations

The last step is for all team members to ensure that they fully understand their assigned responsibilities and how their function affects the responsibilities of other team members. Clarifying expectations involves finding out what you're responsible for doing, determining how your responsibilities support those of other team members, and verifying that team responsibilities align with the team goal.

In this course, you'll learn about establishing team goals, aligning team goals and competencies, and clarifying expectations about individual and team responsibilities.

ESTABLISHING GOALS

Aligning with corporate goals

Psychologist Alfred Adler said "We cannot think, feel, or act without the perception of some goal." Achieving a goal is the main purpose of any team. A clear understanding of that goal is what allows the team to keep focused and on track.

Goals – they're one of the first things established when a team is built.

Individual team members will always have their own goals, but in a team situation, the most important goals are those set for the group as a whole.

These team goals aren't just the sum of what individuals want to achieve. They're shared perceptions of what your team has to achieve together. The greater the understanding of team goals, the more effective your team will be.

When your team is setting goals, you'll need to make sure the goals conform to two main characteristics:

- team goals are linked to the overall corporate goals of your organization, and
- goals are made clear and measurable so that you can use them as meaningful indicators of progress

The first main characteristic of good team goals is that they're clearly **linked to overall corporate goals**. All team goals flow down from the organization's vision and are a part of the business strategy. Each team will have a related – but different – goal that guides that team in carrying out its part in achieving the vision.

Effective organizations maintain a disciplined flow from vision to strategy, to overall goals, to team goals, to measures, to re-

sults, and finally, to team and individual accountability.
Each link ensures that individual efforts are aligned to the overall strategic path and relate back to the organization's vision.
Team goals are most directly aligned with overall corporate goals. For example, an electronics company has an overall corporate goal of producing innovative new products. The design and development project team has an aligned team goal of bringing five new products to market by the end of the fiscal year.
Team goals that are aligned with corporate goals have a number of benefits:
- team members can see how their work directly impacts the organization's progress
- it's easier to sort out and set work priorities, and
- every team member can focus on work that's important to the organization as a whole

Suppose you work for a fitness equipment manufacturer whose vision is to be the number one choice of consumers. One of the overall corporate goals stemming from the vision is to increase consumer satisfaction levels associated with product use.

Question

What would be the best example of a team goal that's in alignment with your company's overall corporate goal of increasing consumer satisfaction with your products?

Options:

1. Use survey data gathered by the Marketing Department to incorporate eight ergonomic features into a new line of products
2. Institute manufacturing efficiencies in order to decrease time-to-market by 15%
3. Reduce energy use by 33% at our manufacturing plants through the implementation of a strategic energy management program

Answer

Option 1: *This is the correct option. Incorporating features at-*

tractive to consumers aligns with your overall corporate goal of increasing customer satisfaction.

Option 2: *This is not a correct option. Manufacturing efficiency is important, but in this case, it doesn't directly align with your corporate goal of increasing customer satisfaction.*

Option 3: *This is not a correct option. Environmental awareness should be a part of your business execution, but in this case, it doesn't directly align with your pursuit of the overall corporate goal of improving customer satisfaction.*

With any team goal, you must be clear how your team's activities will influence the achievement of the overall corporate goal. You must be able to comprehend the piece it plays in achieving the overall goal.

Getting a team in alignment with the organization's goals and strategies takes effort.

You may be tempted to reach for the moon, but too many goals can distract or overwhelm team members.

So, what's important is to understand your corporate goals, and choose one or two team goals that are in direct alignment.

Question

One of the corporate goals of a computer company is to provide customers with superior technical support.

Identify examples of team goals that align with this corporate goal.

Options:
1. The Marketing Department has a team goal of ensuring the information on how to reach technical support is accurate, up to date, and included on the web site and in every computer manual
2. The IT Department has a team goal of increasing system capacity to handle an additional 20% in customer calls
3. The Human Resources Department has a team goal of increasing internal efficiencies to reduce annual costs

by 15%
4. The Logistics Department has a team goal of cutting inventory levels in half

Answer

Option 1: *This is a correct option. The goal of ensuring that customers know how to reach technical support is aligned with the corporate goal of superior service.*

Option 2: *This is a correct option. Increasing the ability of customers to reach a representative is in alignment with the corporate goal of providing superior technical support.*

Option 3: *This is an incorrect option. Departmental efficiency is important, but in this case, the team goal isn't in alignment with providing customers with superior technical support.*

Option 4: *This is an incorrect option. Although inventory levels are a concern, this team goal isn't in alignment with the particular corporate goal of providing customers with superior technical support.*

Clear and measurable goals

So, you've learned that team goals must be aligned with corporate goals. But your team will also need a way to determine whether or not it's making progress toward its goals. Your team will also need to be able to clearly define the moment when goals are achieved. The second main characteristic of good team goals is that they're **clear and measurable**.

For example, your company might have the overall goal of becoming the leader in a particular market. But what does that really mean? How do you know if your team is working toward achieving that goal?

The answer is that you have to characterize your goal in terms of something you can measure. There are different examples of how your company might decide to measure becoming a market leader:

increase the company's market share from 33% to 47%

acquire 10% market share from the company's nearest competitor to place it at number one, and increase the company's retail sales by $3 million

Team goals are more specific than corporate goals because their purpose is to have a core around which you can organize your team efforts.

Team goals always contain clear and achievable objectives. Vague goals are difficult to work toward because they don't specify what it is you have to attain.

Without an idea about quantity, quality, or time, how will you communicate and assess your progress? And how will you know when you've reached your goal?

To determine where they are and where they're going, your team members will need to define all the terms and measurement criteria for each team goal.

For example, if your overall goal is to increase sales, your team will need to define what "increase" means by deciding on a monetary amount, a unit count, a rank comparison, or a percentage.

Question

Now think about a specific team goal that you've worked toward at your own workplace. Did you understand what was needed to achieve that goal?

Options:

1. Yes. It was clear.
2. Pretty much. I had to clarify a few things.
3. My understanding of the goal kept changing.
4. We didn't really have a goal.

Answer

Option 1: *Good. You said the goal was clear to you. This means you knew what had to be achieved and when. But even if you understand, don't hesitate to ask questions to make sure you're on the right path.*

Option 2: *It's good that you clarified your understanding of that team goal. It's important to ask questions to clarify your understanding of the specific objectives your team needs to achieve.*

Option 3: *You said your understanding of the team goal kept changing. This is a sign that the goal was too vague. Team goals need to contain clear and measurable objectives.*

Option 4: *You said your team didn't really have a goal. This means* *that your team didn't have any real purpose, or any means of assessing or measuring success.*

A clear and measurable team goal is quantified with a specific amount or unit of measure, as well as a time frame for completion.

Think back to the example of a fitness equipment manufacturer that had an overall corporate goal of increasing consumer satisfaction levels with the use of its products.

Remember that to create an aligned team goal, the company decided to use survey data gathered by the Marketing Department to incorporate eight ergonomic features into a new line of products.

But the team still needs to make its goal clear and measurable. Although the goal has been quantified with a unit of measure – eight new features – it still needs to be contained by a time frame or deadline so the team can determine not only what's to be done, but by when. The final goal is to incorporate eight ergonomic features into a new line of products **within two years**.

Question

A construction firm has a project team that's working to improve the company's safety record. The team has developed several goals. Identify the best example of a team goal that's clear and measurable.

Options:
1. By the end of this quarter, we will reduce workplace injuries by a minimum of 40%
2. We will develop a regular schedule of preventive maintenance that will reduce accidents and equipment downtime
3. All of the company's heavy equipment will be inspected for compliance with safety standards by the end of the month

Answer

Option 1: *This option is incorrect. The goal is measurable, but there's* no clear indication of how it will be achieved.

Option 2: This option is incorrect. This goal is clear, but it's not characterized in terms of anything that can be measured, such as a target or timeline.

Option 3: This option is correct. This team goal is both clear and measurable. It's clear what has to happen, and there's a timeline for completion.

Analyzing team goals

You've now learned about the two key characteristics of team goals – aligning them with corporate goals, and making them clear and measurable. Here's an opportunity to examine a team's goal-making session as members seek to create team goals that fulfill the requirements.

Imagine a team that works for an international manufacturer of high-quality crystal stemware. The company's vision is to inspire customers through perfection in products and service.

Although the company's products are highly prized by consumers, retail customers have been complaining that there's a high breakage rate in received shipments.

As well, order mix-ups have resulted in more breakage when erroneous shipments are returned to the company.

To deal with the problem, the company has established a corporate goal of assuring shipments to customers are accurate and whole upon receipt.

So three different departments at the crystal stemware company have developed team goals that support the corporate goal.

Follow along with Lee, the director of Human Resources; Mary, who's the manager of the Design division; and Samuel, who runs the Shipping and Receiving Department.

The managers are discussing the team goals they have developed from the corporate goal of assuring shipments are accurate and whole. Follow along as the managers present and analyze their goals.

Lee: This is the team goal we developed: "By year-end, the

EFFECTIVE TEAMWORK

Human Resources Department will establish a full set of guidelines for training employees." What do you think?

Mary: Well, Lee, your goal is measurable and it's clear, but I don't really understand how it's aligned with our corporate goal. How does it relate to breakage?

Lee: I see what you mean. It needs to describe the contents of the training programs. What do you have, Samuel?

Samuel: Our team goal is "The Shipping Department will implement a new performance monitoring system to target process problems, and ensure accuracy in packing orders for shipment."

Lee: Sam, that goal's definitely aligned, and it's clear. But how are you going to measure your progress, or know when you've achieved your goal?

Samuel: Right. I need to make it measurable. OK, Mary, let's hear your goal now.

Mary: You'll like this one, Sam: "The Design Department will reduce breakage in transport by 20% compared to the previous year."

Samuel: Well, that's good news, but how are you going to do that? And by when? Your goal is aligned and measurable, but it isn't at all clear.

Lee: It seems we've all got some revising of goals to do.

What do you think of each team member's assessment about where the goals went wrong? Now, select each manager's name to learn how the goals were revised to be clear, measurable, and aligned with the corporate goal.

Lee

"Now, our team goal is aligned with the corporate goal of reducing breakage. 'By year-end, the Human Resources Department will establish a full set of guidelines for training employees in operational procedures for packaging and handling fragile materials.'"

Mary

"My team made sure our team goal was clear about what we're going to do. 'By year-end, the Design Department will develop a new line of containers that will reduce breakage in transport by 20% compared to the previous year.'"

Samuel

"We had to ensure our team goal was measurable so we could assess our progress. 'The Shipping Department will implement a new performance monitoring system within two months. The system will target process problems and ensure 99% accuracy in packing orders for shipment to customers.'"

Each manager at the meeting revised a team goal to include a missing characteristic of good goals. Lee aligned his team goal with the corporate goal; Mary made sure her goal was clear; and Samuel adjusted his goal so that it was measurable. Now, each of the three teams have goals that are aligned, clear, and measurable.

Case Study: Question 1 of 1

Scenario

For your convenience, the case study is repeated with each question.
Consider an IT company that has developed a new software system for handling e-commerce transactions. After some customers complained that the instructions for using the software are difficult to understand, the company created a corporate goal of improving satisfaction with use of the e-commerce software.
Answer the question about team goals. Question
Various divisions within the company have developed several team goals. Select the best team goal.

Options:

1. Within six weeks, customers will be able to access a live chat feature from the company's web site to discuss questions they have about the new software with customer support representatives
2. The Accounting Department will set up a system so recurring charges are automatically generated, invoiced, and charged to the customer within 30 days
3. The IT Department will create and set up a web site

with information about the software
4. The Publications Department will create a user-friendly manual written at a beginner level for inclusion with each software license

Answer

You should review the characteristics of good team goals.

Option 1: *This option is correct. This choice has all three characteristics of a good team goal. It's clear, measurable, and aligned with the corporate goal.*

Option 2: *This option is incorrect. This goal is measurable and clear, but remember that a good team goal needs to be aligned with the corporate goal.*

Option 3: *This option is incorrect. The goal is aligned, but it isn't clear about what's supposed to happen. What information? Who is the site targeted at?*

Option 4: *This option is incorrect. For a team to gauge success, a goal has to be measurable. This goal needs a completion date.*

Summary

Establishing goals for your team and its members is one of the first and most important things your team will do.

The first main characteristic of having good team goals is that the goals are aligned with overall corporate goals. The next characteristic is that goals are clear about what's going to happen. The third characteristic is that good goals are measurable so that the team can assess progress toward completion.

ALIGNING TEAM ROLES AND COMPETENCIES

Team roles
It's part of human nature to want to influence and control your environment. Accordingly, employees at your organization will have a desire to influence the way things are done and participate in the decision- making process. Teamwork is the best approach to tapping the energy of this potential.

In the first part of building a team, you establish team goals. The second part of building a team is **allocating responsibilities**. This involves aligning team roles and team members' competencies.

This is when you'll build a solid foundation for your team by allocating team roles and responsibilities based on the individual strengths and experience of team members.

When you're allocating responsibilities for your team, you'll need to follow three basic steps. See each step for more information.

Identify the roles on your team
Identifying the roles on your team involves determining what functions need to be created
to complete your team goals.

Assess team members' competencies
Assessing team members' competencies involves determining who has the skill sets

needed to fill team roles.

Assign responsibilities

Assigning responsibilities involves aligning roles and competencies to form a cohesive and synergistic working team.

Matching roles to competencies ensures that team members are doing what they do best. This encourages confidence in the team and in each other.

This confidence leads to trust and to a healthy, mutual respect. And with each confidence-trust cycle, the team enhances its functionality, commitment, and collective capability.

If your team members trust each other to support team goals, follow policies and procedures, and do their job well, they'll be on their way to becoming part of a high-performance team.

Identifying roles

The first step in allocating responsibilities is to **identify the roles on your team**. Because each team is unique, the number and nature of roles within a team depends on the purpose for the team, the nature of the work it's carrying out, the organizational structure, and many other factors.

Roles within a team are like roles in a play. They describe what a person is supposed to do, when they have to do it, and how their part relates to the roles others are playing.

And, just as in the theater, team members need the freedom to interpret their part, but under careful direction.

The benefit of having clear roles and responsibilities is that team members better understand how team goals will be achieved, and how they fit into the big picture.

Because each organization, and each corporate goal, is unique, this topic discusses general roles and responsibilities that are important to the composition of a business team.

When you're building a team, it's important to establish expectations for each team member early on.

This includes determining each team member's responsibilities and what responsibilities team members have to each other. Although it takes time to clarify team roles, you'll save time in the long run because you won't have to deal with conflict over ambiguity and unmet expectations.

The number and nature of roles within your team will depend on a number of factors:

the purpose for forming the team

the goals the team needs to achieve

the organization's business structure the budget and available resources, and the industry in which the team operates

Roles on your team will also vary depending on the type of team. See each type for more information.

Functional team

A **functional team** is organized for an indefinite period of time to provide ongoing support and service in a particular area. If you work within a business unit, you belong to a functional team. Examples include your department – such as IT, Marketing, or Sales – or your management tier – entry-level, junior, or senior.

Project team

A **project team** is organized around a specific goal and timeline. Project teams frequently draw members from different functional units in an organization. Examples include a new product development team, or a specific building construction team.

Contract team

On a **contract team**, some or all of the team members are brought in from outside the company. Organizations use contract teams to save money, or because they require services outside their own core expertise. Examples include an IT team setting up a new computer system, or a security team brought in to conduct an audit.

There are many different types of team roles:

- project or functional manager

- technical experts
- representatives from functional areas
- coaches, and
- workers

A number of typical tasks and responsibilities are associated with team roles. Select each task or responsibility for more information.

Leading the team

Leading the team usually falls to the project or functional manager. These team leaders are responsible for directing and motivating the team, and for ensuring that team goals are strategically aligned with corporate goals.

Providing specific skills and knowledge

Providing specific skills and knowledge is the area of technical and subject matter experts. Their skills allow them to verify the accuracy and precision of information, data, and procedures used by the project team.

Assessing performance and facilitating team meetings

Assessing performance and facilitating team meetings is done by coaches. Coaches mentor new team members and provide training and support. Coaches can be meeting facilitators who steer the decision-making process, or quality control experts who advise the team about keeping on track.

Providing administrative knowledge

Providing administrative knowledge is the responsibility of team representatives from functional areas. These team members are connected to a department or other business unit. They know how to take advantage of the networks through which authority, information, and resources flow in the organization.

Performing general work

General work is a term for everything else that needs to be done on a team. It's driven by the needs of the individual project and team leader. Team members assigned to general work are the supporting players on the team. Their skills may also allow them to step into specific roles, if need be.

A team may have several people filling the same roles. It may also have multiple roles that are filled by one individual. For example, the team leader may also act as a coach. Or a technical expert might also be a representative from a functional area, such as Accounting.

Question

Match each responsibility or task to its associated team role.

Options:

A. Performing general work
B. Providing administrative knowledge
C. Providing specific skills and knowledge
D. Leading the team
E. Providing training and facilitating team meetings

Targets:

1. Supporting team members
2. Representatives from functional areas
3. Technical experts
4. Project or functional manager
5. Coaches

Answer

Supporting team members fill many different functions on a team. Their responsibilities are dictated by the needs of the team leader and by the individual team goals.

Providing administrative knowledge is the responsibility of team representatives from functional areas. For a team to operate efficiently, it has to able to function within the organization's functional networks.

Providing specific skills and knowledge is the area of technical experts. It's important to have team members who can verify the accuracy and precision of information, data, and procedures.

Leading the team usually falls to the project or functional manager. Team leaders are responsible for ensuring that team goals are strategically aligned with corporate goals and for
directing and motivating the team.

Coaches usually provide training and facilitate team meetings. They also mentor new team members and act as meeting facilitators who steer the decision-making process.

Assessing competencies

On any team, you'll have members with different knowledge, talents, skills, and levels of experience. How well your team members do what they do – their competency level – will depend on the nature of your team, as well as the personalities and backgrounds of the people involved.

The second step in allocating responsibilities is to **assess team members' competencies**. You need to find out what skills and behaviors individuals possess, and how these can be put to the best use on the team.

Competencies fall into four general skill areas. See each area for more information.

Leadership skills

Team members with **leadership skills** understand the dynamics of teamwork. They're good at articulating the purpose of the team, and at moving team members toward achieving goals and objectives. Leadership team skills involve strategic thinking, commitment to process improvement, and the ability to inspire and direct others.

Technical skills

Team members with **technical skills** have the expertise to perform specialized tasks. They have particular work-related skills and are service-oriented. Technical team skills involve providing information about specific subject matter and work processes.

Administrative skills

Team members with **administrative skills** are superior organizers. They know how to prioritize and keep track of details. Administrative team skills often involve functional tasks such as budgeting, scheduling, and process management.

Relational skills

Team members with **relational skills** are good at interpersonal communication. They know how to listen, give feedback, and establish trusting relationships with others. Relational team skills involve group decision making, team problem solving, and coaching.

Question
Which competency area do you think you most identify with?
Options:
1. Team members come to me for advice
2. I like procedure, and I'm detail-oriented
3. I'm confident working in my area of expertise
4. I'm good at giving direction and motivating others
Answer
Option 1: You said people often come to you for advice. People who engender trust and who are good communicators have superior relational skills.
Option 2: You said you were detail-oriented. People with superior administrative skills are good at prioritizing and keeping track of details.
Option 3: You said you were confident with your own expertise. People with specific expertise usually have good technical skills.
Option 4: You said you were good at giving direction and motivating others. People with leadership skills have an understanding of the big picture and cultivate a clear sense of direction that guides everyone else.

Complementary skills are important on a team because they allow you to take advantage of a greater range of talent and knowledge.

Of course, many people have multiple competencies. For example, you may have strong relational skills, but also be very organized and knowledgeable about your job.

When your team members have multiple competencies, it's likely they'll be able to perform different functions and that they may have similar or overlapping skills.

When you're building a team, the most important thing isn't

EFFECTIVE TEAMWORK

what every individual does best, but what's the best combination of competencies. You'll have to weigh your own skills and those of your team members to find the best overall balance.

Question
Match the four competency areas with their defining characteristics.

Options:
A. Leadership skills
B. Administrative skills C. Technical skills
D. Relational skills

Targets:
1. This area includes understanding the dynamics of teamwork, articulating goals, and directing team members toward achieving objectives
2. This area includes functional tasks such as budgeting, scheduling, and process management
3. This area includes specific work-related skills, and the provision of information and expertise about work processes
4. This area includes group decision making, team problem solving, meeting facilitation, and coaching

Answer
Leadership skills involve strategic thinking, commitment to process improvement, and the ability to inspire and direct others.
Administrative skills involve organizing, prioritizing, and keeping track of details.
Technical skills involve providing the particular skills and expertise needed to perform specialized tasks.
Relational skills involve interpersonal communication such as listening, giving feedback, and establishing trusting relationships with others.

Assigning responsibilities
The last step in allocating responsibilities is to **assign responsibilities based on competencies**. This involves analyzing the

roles on the team and filling them with team members who have the best competencies for those roles.

See the typical team roles for more about the competencies that align with each.

Managers
Project or functional managers are the team leaders. They require good leadership skills to guide and manage their team.

Technical experts
Technical experts provide specific knowledge to the team. They require good technical skills.

Coaches
Coaches facilitate progress by mentoring and steering the team. They require good relational skills.

Representatives from functional areas
Representatives from functional areas provide functional skills and knowledge. They require good administrative skills.

Workers
Workers perform all kinds of tasks. A team needs a good mix of workers with talents in all four skill areas – leadership, technical, relational, and administrative.

Assigning roles can be more complicated than it seems.

What if you have team members who could fill a number of different roles?

Or what if you have roles that none of your team members seem competent to perform?

When you're assigning roles on a team, a decision matrix can help you assess competencies to create a balanced team. A decision matrix is a valuable evaluation tool for prioritizing a list of options.

For example, say you work for a furniture manufacturer. You're in charge of new product development, and you're putting together a team to take an ergonomically designed office chair from concept through to commercialization.

In this case, you could use a matrix for each skill area to assess

EFFECTIVE TEAMWORK

your potential team members' suitability for team roles.
For instance, what if you needed a project manager? In this case, you'd be dealing with leadership skills.
To assess your team members' leadership skills, you would follow three steps to create a simple decision matrix. Select each step, in order, for more information.

Step 1: Create a table
Create a table that has the team member names down the left column and particular leadership skills you need for your project across the top row.
This decision matrix is a table with seven columns representing skills and six rows representing team members. The skill columns are filled in with these skills: strategic thinker, committed to process improvement, inspires others, articulate, good goal-setter, understands dynamics of teamwork, and gives good direction.
The team member rows are filled in with the team member names: Janet, Norm, David, Shelley, Jia, and Omar.

Step 2: Assess team members
Now you need to decide on a rating scale with corresponding values. You could use S (strong) with a value of two, A (average), with a value of one, and W (weak), with a value of zero. Add the ratings to intersecting cells to signify which team members possess which competencies.
A rating has been added to each cell at the intersection of a skill column and a team member row. The ratings are strong, average, or weak. Strong ratings are worth 2, average ratings are worth 1, and weak ratings are worth 0.

Step 3: Assign responsibilities
Determine the team member for the role based on the total score of their skills.
Janet's score adds up to 10. Norm's score is 9.
David's score is 12. Shelley's score is 13.
Jia's score is 9. Omar's score is 6.
Shelley's score of 13 is the highest among these team members.

It's important to create a decision matrix for each skill area – leadership, technical, relational, and administrative. In the example of the project team at a furniture manufacturer, the decision matrix for leadership competencies showed that Shelley had the highest score. Do you think this means that she would be the best team leader?

Shelley would make a good team leader. But what if your decision matrix for technical skills showed that Shelley rated much higher than anyone else in that area?

David scored almost as high as Shelley for leadership skills. In this case, you might decide that the team would be better off with David as the team leader and Shelley as a technical expert. Remember, decisions should be based on what's good for the team as a whole.

One consideration when allocating team roles is that they can be mixed and matched, depending on the needs of your team and its mix of competencies.

For example, on many teams, the team leader may also act as a coach – assessing progress or mentoring new team members. But what if the practical workload of leading the team becomes too heavy for the team leader to continue devoting time to coaching?

If you know the competencies of your team members, you can find a worker who has the relational skills to take on the coaching role, either permanently or until the team leader has time again.

Case Study: Question 1 of 4

Scenario

For your convenience, the case study is repeated with each question.

You work for a software company that develops and markets cutting-edge computer games. You are to select several team members to fill roles on a project team tasked with creating a new game. You have compiled notes on five team members that will help you assess their skills and decide which team roles they'd be best suited for.

Answer each question about aligning team roles and competencies.

Question

Which team member would make the best team leader?

Options:

1. Anna
2. Bob
3. Aldo
4. Eden
5. Marcy

Answer

Option 1: This is the correct option. Team leaders have good leadership skills. Anna's leadership strengths are strategic thinking, team dynamics, and the ability to inspire and direct others.

Option 2: This option is incorrect. Bob's skills aren't suited to being a team leader.

Option 3: This option is incorrect. Aldo's competencies don't align with leadership skills.

Option 4: This option is incorrect. Eden would not be the best choice for team leader.

Option 5: This option is incorrect. Although Marcy has a commitment to process improvement, Anna has better leadership skills.

Case Study: Question 2 of 4

Scenario

For your convenience, the case study is repeated with each question.

You work for a software company that develops and markets cutting-edge computer games. You are to select several team members to fill roles on a project team tasked with creating a new game. You have compiled notes on five team members that will help you assess their skills and decide which team roles they'd be best suited for.

Answer each question about aligning team roles and competencies. Question

The team needs someone who can advise members about the

technical issues of game design.

Which team member would make the best technical expert?

Options:

1. Anna 2. Bob 3. Aldo 4. Eden 5. Marcy

Answer

Option 1: This option is incorrect. Anna has some technical skills, but her greatest strengths are in a different skill area.

Option 2: This option is incorrect. Bob would be better suited to a role that doesn't need technical skills.

Option 3: This option is incorrect. Aldo doesn't possess the specialized skills needed to be a technical expert.

Option 4: This is the correct option. Technical experts have good technical skills. Eden's technical strengths are her expert knowledge of game creation technologies and techniques, and her service-oriented approach to helping fellow team members.

Option 5: This option is incorrect. Marcy has some specific technical knowledge, but she isn't the best overall choice as a technical expert.

Case Study: Question 3 of 4

Scenario

For your convenience, the case study is repeated with each question.

You work for a software company that develops and markets cutting-edge computer games. You are to select several team members to fill roles on a project team tasked with creating a new game. You have compiled notes on five team members that will help you assess their skills and decide which team roles they'd be best suited for.

Answer each question about aligning team roles and competencies. Question

The project team needs a person who can liaise with the functional departments at the company.

Which team member would make the best functional representative on the team?

Options:

1. Anna 2. Bob 3. Aldo 4. Eden 5. Marcy

Answer

Option 1: This option is incorrect. Although Anna is connected to a functional department, her strongest skills are in a different skill area.

Option 2: This is the correct option. Functional representatives have good administrative skills. The fact that Bob is organized, is detail-oriented, and understands the functional structure of the company makes him the best choice as a functional representative on the project team.

Option 3: This option is incorrect. Aldo is a good communicator, but his main strengths lie in a different skill area.

Option 4: This option is incorrect. Eden likes to work somewhat independently. She wouldn't be the best choice for a functional representative.

Option 5: This option is incorrect. Marcy has good all-around skills, but she wouldn't be the best person to act as the team's functional representative.

Case Study: Question 4 of 4

Scenario

For your convenience, the case study is repeated with each question.
You work for a software company that develops and markets cutting-edge computer games. You are to select several team members to fill roles on a project team tasked with creating a new game. You have compiled notes on five team members that will help you assess their skills and decide which team roles they'd be best suited for.

Answer each question about aligning team roles and competencies. Question
The project team needs someone to facilitate meetings and assess the performance of team members.
Which team member would make the best coach?
Options:
1. Anna
2. Bob

3. Aldo
4. Eden
5. Marcy Answer

Option 1: This option is incorrect. Anna does have good communication skills, but her particular skills mean she's best suited for a different role on the team.

Option 2: This option is incorrect. Bob isn't the best choice as a coach.

Option 3: This is the correct option. Coaches have good relational skills. Aldo is skilled at
communication, conflict resolution, and providing feedback.

Option 4: This option is incorrect. Eden has specific skills that aren't relational in nature. She wouldn't be a good choice as a coach.

Option 5: This option is incorrect. Marcy likes to provide her opinion, but there's no indication she's a good listener. She wouldn't be the best choice as a coach.

Summary

The second part of building a team is allocating responsibilities. This involves aligning team roles and team members' competencies.

The three steps in allocating responsibilities are to identify the roles on your team, assess team members' competencies, and assign responsibilities to team members based on their competencies.

CLARIFYING EXPECTATIONS

Seeking clarification

Imagine that your team leader hands you a simple goal – to train a new team member. Two weeks later, your leader tells you he isn't pleased with the results. You thought you did a thorough job covering the way the team works. But your team leader wanted the new recruit trained on a specific piece of software. He assumed you would know that. You feel frustrated and doomed to failure. What happened?

What happened was that you and your team leader had different expectations of what was supposed to happen when a new team member was trained.

An expectation is simply an assumption about how things are going to turn out. For example, you might think you know how someone will behave, how something should be done, or how a situation will resolve itself.

You might be surprised and upset when something happens that doesn't meet your expectations.

Your team is simply a group of individuals brought together to achieve a goal. And each individual on that team may have different expectations of what has to happen to reach that goal. When you're working on a team, it's important to **clarify expectations** about the nature of each person's involvement in reaching the goal. This means making sure everyone understands team roles and responsibilities. Put simply, people should know what to do, and how to do it.

Clarifying expectations is important because it removes misunderstanding and clears up ambiguity about how your team works.

Every member of a team has the responsibility to clarify expectations. The team leader needs to clearly spell out roles and responsibilities.

And team members also need to take the initiative to find out exactly what expectations the team leader has of them.

You'll need to clarify expectations in two basic categories. See each category to learn more.

General

General expectations include ideas about communication, compensation, relationships, and corporate culture.

Task

Task expectations involve ideas about what has to be achieved, who has to achieve it, and what steps need to be taken to reach completion.

Clarification is important for a number of reasons:
- it defines the individual roles, responsibilities, tasks, and functions each team member is expected to perform
- it helps you to understand specific procedures or standards that must be followed
- it ensures that team members who share tasks are clear on their parts, and
- it allows the team to identify the interdependence of tasks, and determine priorities

Suppose you're on a team that's working on a historical restoration project. Alex, the team leader, is upset because the project is over budget. Follow along as Alex discusses the issue with Terry, the structural engineer, and Val, the architect.

Alex: We're only midway through the project and we're well over budget. It seems that we've ordered and paid for more materials than we need for this job. Also, a check to one of our suppliers bounced. What's going on?

Alex is concerned.
Terry: I ordered the construction materials, but it seems Val didn't ask me, and she ordered them too.
Terry is unhappy.
Val: That's because it was my job. I always do the ordering. *Val is annoyed.*
Terry: And how was I supposed to know that, Val? And why is it your job?
Terry is annoyed.
Alex: Neither of you should be doing any ordering until you check with me. We have procedures for ordering materials and paying invoices that must be followed.
Alex is serious.
Terry: Where are these procedures? At the back of a locked filing cabinet in your office?
Terry is upset
Val: And someone had to get those supplies here, otherwise our timeline would've been shot.
Val is annoyed.
Terry: What timeline?
Terry is shocked.
Alex: I'm getting a headache. *Alex looks pained.*

The renovation project team was over budget because team members hadn't clarified expectations.

As team leader, Alex hadn't defined responsibilities for his team members or made sure they knew about policies and procedures. As well, Terry and Val had made assumptions about what they were supposed to do, rather than clarifying roles with each other and with Alex.

It's clear from this example that no matter what your position on a team, you need to know what's expected from you in order to move ahead in the right strategic direction.

Nothing can guarantee perfection. But seeking clarification about your expectations, and clarifying team members' expectations about your responsibilities, will ensure that your strategic path is clear and that you're doing all you can to achieve success.

Question

Why is it important to seek clarification about expectations?

Options:
1. Your expectations determine how you carry out tasks, so it's important they match your manager's expectations
2. It allows the team to identify the interdependence of tasks, and determine priorities
3. It ensures team members responsible for shared tasks are clear on their part
4. It helps individuals to understand specific procedures or standards that must be followed
5. It ensures that your project or initiative meets its team goal
6. It helps you avoid being blamed for other people's mistakes

Answer

You'll need to review the importance of seeking clarification.

Option 1: This option is correct. Clarifying expectations creates a common understanding about what team members are expected to do, and how they're expected to perform.

Option 2: This option is correct. Team members need to know how their activities will impact the efforts of others on the team.

Option 3: This option is correct. Clarifying shared tasks can help team members from missing steps or duplicating efforts.

Option 4: This option is correct. Team members can't follow procedures or standards they don't know about.

Option 5: This option is incorrect. Nothing can guarantee perfection, but seeking clarification will ensure that you're doing all you can to achieve success.

Option 6: This option is incorrect. Team members should work together to clarify understanding about the path to reaching the team goal.

Understanding expectations

A good team leader takes the time to explain what's required of team members, but nobody can anticipate everything they'll need to know. The best way to clarify expectations is to ask questions.

If you're not 100% sure of what you need to do, and what you're accountable for, you'll need to find answers early on in your project or initiative.

Clarifying expectations involves three steps:
1. find out what you're responsible for
2. determine how your responsibilities support other team members, and
3. verify that team responsibilities align with the goal

The first step in clarifying expectations is to **find out what you're responsible for**. At the first opportunity, tell your team that you'd like to discuss responsibilities, or ask your team leader to explain what your responsibilities should be. By asking questions at this stage, you'll determine exactly what's expected of you. You won't miss anything important, and you won't end up doing someone else's work.

What if team members from the historical renovation project made sure to ask questions to find out what their responsibilities were? Follow along for examples of the questions they might ask.

Alex: Has everyone read the procedures that have to be followed for ordering materials and paying invoices? Does anyone have any questions?

Terry: I'd like to clarify who's responsible for dealing with suppliers. Will it be me, as the project engineer?

Val: I assumed I'd be ordering materials. Do you want me to make up my orders and give them to Terry?

Alex: Val, you can give your orders to Terry. To avoid ordering more than we need, he can compile a master list and then submit it to me as project leader as outlined in our procedures.

The second step in clarifying expectations is to **determine**

how your responsibilities support other team members. You'll need to ask questions and be available to answer questions from your team members.

Working toward a team goal is a shared effort. Your fellow team members rely on you to do your work correctly and on time so that they can do their own. For example, you may have to hand off deliverables to someone else before that person can complete a task. Any delay you create will affect the ability of your teammates to meet their deadlines.

By asking questions at this stage, you'll be able to determine the interdependencies of tasks and responsibilities, and how those dependencies affect overall timelines.

Follow along as team members from the historical renovation project ask questions about how their responsibilities support other team members.

Alex: Now that we've reviewed our responsibilities, does anyone have any questions about how you're going to be working together?

Terry: Alex, will the rest of the materials be delivered to the site by the end of the month? If they aren't here, we'll have to delay the start of plastering.

Terry is pleasant.

Val: I'm glad you asked about that. If you delay the plastering, it'll affect when we can begin the painting. Will that be a problem?

Alex: Yes. The decorators can't start until the painting is finished. Also, Marketing has arranged for photographs to be taken of the finished project. They need the photos to update the brochure and web site before the opening on June 15.

Terry: So as I understand it, the delivery of the materials by month's end is an important part of our schedule. Is that correct?

Alex: Yes. I'll make sure there's no delay, so neither of your timelines will be affected. Marketing can complete their responsibilities, and the opening date won't be affected.

The last step in clarifying expectations is to **verify that team**

responsibilities align with the goal. In the first two steps, you determined what your responsibilities were, and how they meshed with the
responsibilities of other team members. Now, your team will commit to one course of action.

By asking questions at this stage, you'll clarify how all the responsibilities together will form a strategic path leading toward the successful completion of the team's goal.

Follow along as team members ask questions about responsibilities for meeting the goal of the historical renovation project.

Alex: Let's make sure we all understand the big picture. Our goal is to restore the building to a historically accurate appearance and structural configuration by June 15, when it opens to the public. Are there any questions?

Terry: Yes. We have an opportunity to buy some narrow hardwood flooring. It would save us some money, if we got it now. Should I pursue the purchase?

Val: Well, the goal is to restore the original appearance of the house. That means wide-plank flooring.

Alex: Thanks, Val. Terry, don't pursue the purchase.

Val: There are bound to be a lot of decisions about historical accuracy, and we can't anticipate them all. I'll take on the responsibility of acting as intermediary if any questions come up about architectural details. Is this agreed?

Terry: Yes. It'll save us time and rework, if we know who to check with about historical accuracy.

Question
Which are the best examples of questions that team members might ask to clarify expectations?
Options:
1. "Who will be inputting the data I'm collecting?"
2. "As team leader, will I be responsible for managing the project timeline?"
3. "Will these estimated activity durations allow our team to meet the project deadline?"

4. "I'm clear on my responsibilities. Do the rest of you want to continue on while I head back to the office?"
   5. "We've talked about our team goal, but we haven't determined individual responsibilities."

Answer

Option 1: *This option is correct. Asking questions will help you determine how your responsibilities fit in with other team members' responsibilities.*

Option 2: *This option is correct. You need to ask questions to find out what you're responsible for on the team so you won't miss anything, or end up doing the wrong job.*

Option 3: *This option is correct. You need to seek clarification of how the collective responsibilities of the team fit with the team's goal.*

Option 4: *This option is incorrect. Even if you're clear on your responsibilities, you should be available to answer questions from your fellow team members. They also need clarification.*

Option 5: *This option is incorrect. Just making a general statement isn't going to help clarify much. It's important to ask questions about the specific information you're seeking. What do you want to know?*

Summary

Clarifying expectations about the nature of each person's involvement in reaching the team goal is important. Every member of a team has the responsibility to clarify expectations, and the best way to do this is by asking questions.

Clarifying expectations involves three steps. First, find out what you're responsible for. Next, determine how your responsibilities support other team members. Finally, verify that collective team responsibilities align with the goal of your project or initiative.

ELEMENTS OF A COHESIVE TEAM

Teams are a familiar concept. Since childhood, most people have been a member of one team or another, from sports teams to work teams. Being part of a team means working with others toward a common goal. Team cohesiveness – how bound together the team members are – determines how effective the team will be, particularly in responding to outside pressures.

Cohesion benefits all teams regardless of structure, culture, or task. Military squads or platoons are teams that require a strong team cohesion as they face the rigors of combat.

Emergency response teams must be able to work together flawlessly to save lives. Deep sea divers and space exploration teams are examples of teams where cohesion is vital for safety and performance in extreme environments.

Similarly, business teams that are under pressure to perform at a high level must be tightly bound together to work closely and efficiently toward common goals.

What does it mean when a team is cohesive? A cohesive team has several characteristics:

team members cooperate with each other to reach their goals
there is mutual trust and respect
team members focus on achievement and improvement
team morale is high and commitment is strong, and
team members use "we," not "I," when talking about getting the job done

What is the importance of team identity? Consider the most cohesive team you have ever been a part of. Were team members easily distinguished from non-team members?

Cohesive teams have a strong sense of team identity. Team members recognize what makes the team special, its strengths, and its goals, and they give the team greater commitment and effort.

Often, teams are distinguished by outward symbols such as uniforms, dress codes, customs, and rituals. Work teams often wear team T-shirts and hats to identify themselves as part of a particular team. This outward identification helps members see themselves as mutually accountable for results.

Three basic elements work together to build a cohesive team: communication, cooperation, and trust. These three elements do not stand alone. For example, building trust depends on good communication and a cooperative spirit.

Similarly, a high degree of trust may be vital before cooperation is possible, depending on the situation or the nature of the task. Consider an international committee charged with developing economic policies. Team members may need to overcome competing priorities and cultural differences and establish trust before they can achieve a degree of cooperation.

In this course, you'll explore the three strands of the cord that intertwine to create a cohesive team:

communication, cooperation, and trust. You'll learn to recognize some of the indicators that point to a lack of cohesion and the elements they signify are most lacking. You'll also learn to apply the strategies for building trust, improving communication, and increasing cooperation to improve overall team cohesion.

COMMUNICATION WITHIN THE TEAM

Responding positively

Good communication – along with cooperation and trust – are the threads that bind a team into a cohesive unit. Without good communication, cooperation and trust are unlikely to develop. In a cohesive team, communication is clear and positive, and ideas flow freely.

Poor communication, on the other hand, leads to misunderstandings, hurt feelings, missed opportunities, and conflict.

If people on your team take offense quickly, make avoidable mistakes, and are frequently in conflict, your team may have communication problems.

If your team members are hesitant to say what they mean because other team members are "touchy," communication on your team isn't as good as it should be.

You can use three overall strategies to improve communication and build a cohesive team: respond positively, demonstrate a sense of partnership, and talk to each other.

Sometimes a coworker says something offensive or ambiguous that could be taken as an insult or a slight. When that happens, there are three useful ways to respond positively and build a cohesive team:

- Start by thinking the speaker didn't mean to offend. Assume good intentions and don't get defensive. If you assume the worst, you'll probably get it.
- Don't retaliate. Going on the offensive will just escalate the negative part of the conversation. Rather than saying

"Now wait a minute. What do you mean by that?" reply in a way that's neutral, or better yet, positive.
- Go beyond simply avoiding a negative response and say something positive that helps the team move forward.

Question

One of your teammates says to you, "I'm this team's number one producer. Don't even bother trying to beat me."
Which response do you think would be the most effective?

Options:

1. "I think we should set aside our competitiveness."
2. "You're right. But we're both top producers. If we work together and share our knowledge and resources, we'll make our team number one."
3. "Is that a challenge? Why, I think it is. You're on!" Answer

Option 1: This option is incorrect. You didn't get defensive, retaliate, or rise to the challenge. But, on the other hand, you could have been more proactive by assuming good intentions and redirecting the energy toward team success.

Option 2: This is the correct option. You're being proactive in trying to turn a competitive relationship into a collaborative one that'll increase team cohesiveness. You express the belief that the teammate was trying to be positive about reaching team goals.

Option 3: This option is incorrect. You may be tempted to go this route. It's most likely the response closest to your gut reaction. But it'll harm the team in the long run. And there's really no such thing as a "healthy competition" when team cohesiveness is the goal. This approach puts your needs first, not the team's.

Demonstrating a sense of partnership

Brainstorming, problem solving, and decision making require the free flow of ideas, and when you and your teammates put forth your ideas, you make yourselves vulnerable. As your ideas, beliefs, and opinions are laid bare and criticized, this criticism can feel like a personal attack.

The second strategy to improve team communication is to demonstrate a sense of partnership. Creating a sense of partner-

EFFECTIVE TEAMWORK

ship will ease or prevent feelings of personal attack. To build cohesiveness in this way, you should keep a couple of simple communication tips in mind:

Try to communicate your sense of partnership. Let your teammates know you look forward to working with them, and you value their opinions and ideas.

Express your desire to work together on problems and resolve any issues as a team.

Mark leads a highly cohesive team working on a marketing project. Follow along to learn how a cohesive team's communication reflects a sense of partnership.

Mark: Liz, you were in charge of coming up with the project name and a rough plan for us to discuss today, right?

LIz: That's right. I've passed out some notes and a list of some initial ideas that Jerry and I brainstormed last night.

Ellie: I really like your idea of using contractors for phone promotion. How can I help? Would you like me to get you some information on companies that do that sort of work?

Liz: That would be great. I know you're really experienced in that area, and I'd feel confident in whoever you'd recommend.

Mark: Liz, it appears you'll need more resources for the marketing research. Maybe you could come along and make a presentation to the board members when I try to get their approval.

Ellie: With you two representing us, we'll surely get the resources. You can count on me to help you prepare.

Mark's team members are focused on partnering and working as a team. They make it clear in their conversation that they all value each other's input. If they had shown signs of preferring to work individually, that might be an indicator of communication problems related to partnering.

Question

Based on your personal experience, which team behaviors indicate problems with communication?
Options:
    1. To avoid giving offense, team members tend to tread

lightly when discussing each other's ideas
2. The team has a history of missed opportunities and mistakes that could have been avoided
3. Several people on the team seem quiet and standoffish
4. One or two assertive individuals seem to perform better than others
5. One team member in particular volunteers for every assignment

Answer

Option 1: *This is a correct option. When people are afraid that others will take offense, past conflict has probably led to a communication problem.*

Option 2: *This is a correct option. Missed opportunities and mistakes indicate poor*
communication. The team atmosphere probably doesn't allow for the free and easy exchange of ideas.

Option 3: *This is a correct option. If some team members seem like loners, you may need to pay more attention to getting people to talk to one another.*

Option 4: *This is an incorrect option. It's natural for some members to excel. This doesn't reflect poor communication as long as their behavior is collaborative rather than competitive.*

Option 5: *This is an incorrect option. An eager volunteer doesn't indicate a communication problem as long as the person is ready and willing to work with others.*

Talking to each other

A third strategy for helping to build cohesiveness on your team is to simply get your people to talk to each other.

For social individuals, team members who have things in common, or those who are already friends, this will probably come easily.

For others, keeping lines of communication open and flowing may be more difficult.

When some team members don't get fully involved in the discussion and aren't social with other members, you may have a communication problem. It's important to find ways to bring these introverts into the normal conversational flow of the team.

To get people talking to each other, you need to help them get to know each other on a personal basis.

Teams are often under pressure to meet deadlines, and time can be a precious commodity. But it's important to devote some of that time to building cohesiveness. You need to allow some time for casual conversation and try to get everyone to participate.

To bring people into the conversation and get them talking, you may need to figure out what they're interested in and discuss it.

Frank is a team lead whose team has a cohesiveness problem. After holding several workshops on positive team communication, things got a little better, but two of his team members, Jake and Lily, rarely participate in team discussion. They tend to be quiet, passive observers. Frank tries to address this by making time before team meetings to strike up short conversations, just enough to show interest and make Jake and Lily feel connected. As a result, they begin to join in more with the team dialog.

Question

Which are examples of communicating in ways that build a cohesive team?

Options:

1. When Antonio said, "I'm excited to work with the new product line you've developed. It's way better than your old one," Olga said, "Thanks, I think it will do well for us."
2. Sumie said, "Don't struggle with that presentation by yourself. If we all work on it together, it will go faster and easier, and make us a stronger team."
3. At the start of each team meeting, the leader allows for about five minutes of casual conversation before settling down to business.

4. To encourage productivity, the team's top producer challenged the rest of the team to beat his sales scores.
5. The team leader said, "Omar, you really should participate more in meetings. I've noticed you're always very quiet."

Answer

Option 1: *This is a correct option. Assuming the best intentions and responding positively to questionable remarks is a way to build cohesion.*

Option 2: *This is a correct option. Cohesion is increased when team members communicate a willingness to partner with their teammates.*

Option 3: *This is a correct option. Keeping communication flowing helps make a cohesive team. Providing opportunities to get everyone involved is important.*

Option 4: *This is an incorrect option. The idea of healthy competition is, for the most part, a myth. Collaboration is what builds team cohesion, not competitiveness.*

Option 5: *This is an incorrect option. Simply telling loners to stop acting the way they do isn't likely to change team communication for the better.*

Summary

To increase your team's cohesiveness, some communication methods are more effective than others. Keep things positive by assuming your teammates just want what's best for the team and not rising to the bait of aggressive or ambiguous remarks. Going the extra step of focusing on team progress is even better for building cohesion.

Express your desire to work together and show respect for the ideas of others to help create a sense of partnership. To draw people into the overall team conversation, you can work on getting to know them on a personal basis.

THE IMPORTANCE OF COOPERATION TO TEAM SUCCESS

Putting the team's needs first
Consider a family where mom works at a high-paying job she enjoys. Dad works nights as a professional musician, taking care of the younger kids and the house during the day. The teenage son has a part-time job. The daughter wins a scholarship to a prestigious college. Families are teams. They work together on the task of living, and they celebrate each other's contributions as good for the team. Cooperation is important to make the family a cohesive unit.

Team members need to cooperate to get the job done, whatever that job may be. You can apply three simple strategies to promote cooperation among your team members:

when deciding how to approach work, put the team's needs first because, in the long run, that's what's best for you too

accept and perform unpleasant tasks with a positive attitude and try to get others to do the same, and

discourage competition, which is usually unhealthy for building a cohesive team

To put the team's needs first, it's best to develop the habit of acting unselfishly. When someone asks you to go above and beyond your own responsibilities, your answer should be "yes."

Say, for example, one of your coworkers is in charge of scheduling. She asks you to keep the rest of the people on the team up to date on a particular issue as it develops. The task involves sending an e-mail once in a while.

It's not truly your job, and you would be well within your rights to say "no." But the task isn't too difficult and it's only for a short period of time. If you want a cohesive team, don't hesitate; just say "yes."

If you or someone on your team has a "no way, that's not my job" attitude when faced with these kinds of requests, cooperation within the team isn't very healthy.

Proactively searching for ways to help the team is another effective strategy for increasing cooperation and building cohesion. To be proactive means finding ways to help the team that go beyond simply reacting to a need or an assignment. If you have spare time, offer to help others on the team. Or you could identify and pre-emptively tackle a potential problem in order to make the team's work easier in the long run.

Question

What would you say if your boss asked you to go out of town on a business trip rather than asking a teammate whose personal obligations make it more difficult to travel? You don't think it's fair, because this is the third time in a row you've been asked to travel out of town. But you go anyway for the good of the team. Which response do you think would be the most effective?

Options:
1. "I knew this was a possibility. I want the team to succeed, and in the grand scheme of things, this is a small sacrifice."
2. "I knew this was a possibility. As the saying goes, this too shall pass. I'll do it for the team, but I don't have to pretend to like it. You're really going to owe me one."

Answer

Option 1: Good. This is the best response. You're letting your boss know that going out of town again isn't your number one choice, but the results will be worth it. When your attitude is good about things like this, other team members will pick up on it, and team cohesive-

ness will increase.

Option 2: *This is a fair response. You have a right to let your boss know you aren't thrilled. But it's not the best response because even though you're putting the team's needs ahead of your own, you're making it clear you don't really want to. Be a little more positive to contribute to a sense of cooperation.*

Accepting unpleasant tasks positively

Most people know that working with others on a team involves accepting your share of unpleasant tasks. But an important strategy for building cooperation is to take on those tasks with a positive attitude.

If you accept the task with a smile instead of a grumble, you'll demonstrate that the team's needs are more important than your own. Others will notice your actions and follow suit, creating a more cooperative atmosphere.

It's clear that if team members most often respond to an unpleasant task by trying to get out of it or by just saying "no," there's a lack of cooperation. But simply agreeing to perform an unwanted task doesn't guarantee a cooperative environment. If people say "yes" but continue to complain about having to perform the task, your team may have cooperation issues.

Consider this situation. Andrew and Joan work in the Accounting Department of a parts manufacturer. Every month, someone in the department has to make follow-up calls to customers who are behind in their payments. It's unpleasant work that no one enjoys.

Andrew always tries to pass off the job to someone else. He makes it obvious that he'll be unhappy if he gets stuck doing it. Sometimes others take over the task just to avoid listening to his complaints.

Joan, on the other hand, accepts the rotating duty with a smile. Her fellow team members kid her about getting stuck with the task, but they also help whenever they can. And when the job is done, they all go out to lunch to celebrate.

Question

Which actions indicate a problem with cooperation?

Options:
1. The team lead keeps the best clients for himself and assigns the lower-dollar accounts to the rest of the team.
2. Brett immediately agreed to take on the maintenance project for the good of the team, but he spends all his time complaining about it.
3. Martha was busy but she knew the team was going to need more information on database management software. She gathered the necessary information before the meeting.
4. Matsuri always gives credit to others for their contributions to the team success and is quick to say that she enjoys working with them.

Answer

Option 1: This is a correct option. The team lead is not putting the team's needs ahead of his own. His actions demonstrate he doesn't understand how cooperation works at all.

Option 2: This is a correct option. Grumbling about taking on unpleasant tasks is an indicator that Brett has failed to do so with a positive attitude.

Option 3: This is an incorrect option. Proactively taking on tasks that will benefit the team puts the team's needs first and helps build a cooperative environment.

Option 4: This is an incorrect option. Telling others you enjoy working with them isn't a problem indicator, but rather a healthy way to promote cooperation on the team.

Discouraging competition

Consider a situation where all 50 employees in a department interview for a particularly attractive management position. Applicants who meet each other in the waiting area wish each other luck, but they don't really mean it. In the end, one person gets the job. That's competition for you. Someone wins, and everyone else loses. To build cohesion, you must discourage competition.

Some corporate management styles use competition as a motivator, offering rewards if an individual or a team becomes the number one performer or meets certain goals.

Some corporate cultures encourage competition, some tasks lend themselves to it, and some individuals are just naturally competitive.

But to the extent that competition among team members inhibits cooperation, it works against team efforts and affects team cohesiveness.

By definition, teams are made up of members who collaborate – that is, they work for a mutual win, not individual advancement. If another team member is out for personal advantage, how can you trust that person to do what's good for the team?

When members show signs of competitiveness – either overtly by challenging others on the team or in more subtle ways – both cooperation and cohesion are at risk. Your strategies in this case should be to consider the team's success as your own and encourage others to adopt a collaborative approach.

See the suggested behaviors to learn how to guard against the damaging effects of competition.

Consider the team's success as your own

If you act as if the team's overall well-being and success are the measure of your personal success, competitiveness is out the door. The belief that the eventual success of the team is more important than small individual successes is a solid foundation for cooperation. It will encourage the sharing of resources and knowledge.

Encourage others to adopt a collaborative approach

Encourage your fellow team members to adopt a collaborative approach to the team's work. Rather than competing with someone on your team, ask that person to work with you. When the two of you combine your resources and knowledge, you'll make the team stronger. Your teammates are your partners, not your enemies. Demonstrate your appreciation of your teammates and make sure to give credit when it's due.

When Warren notices his teammates keeping track of their daily statistics and betting on who will hit the highest total for the week, he takes them aside. He suggests a more constructive way to ensure the team will hit its overall goals. He points out that since the eventual success of the team is what's important, team members should be sharing resources and knowledge to make that happen.

Question
Vera leads a municipal task force that's working on the affordable housing shortage. To build a strong team, she needs to promote cooperation.
Which statements reflect strategies for increasing cooperation?
Options:
1. "Whenever I'm caught up on my work, I check with my team members to find out if anybody could use a hand. Lately, I've noticed others doing the same thing."
2. "Nobody wanted the task of scheduling vacations. But, it needed to be done, so I jumped right in. I joked that at least I could ensure everyone would be in town for the company party."
3. "The previous team leader ran a weekly contest, rewarding the employee who had the lowest expenses. I immediately got rid of that policy."
4. "Management plans to pay quarterly bonuses starting next year. I'm keeping that information to myself for now. Maybe someday I can use the news to ease tension and build cohesion."
5. "Two team members complained constantly about having to travel abroad together to learn about other housing programs. I encouraged them to vent their frustrations."

Answer

Option 1: *This is a correct option. Being proactive in furthering the team's work is a way to build cooperation. By putting team needs above your own, you set the tone for increased cooperation.*

Option 2: *This is a correct option. You can build a sense of cooperation by accepting unpleasant tasks. And it's even better to do so in a positive way that shows you're willing to sacrifice a little for the good of the team.*

Option 3: *This is a correct option. Teams are collaborative by definition. Although often used as a motivator, competition works against cooperation, and in most cases, it isn't good for the team.*

Option 4: *This is an incorrect option. Vera isn't promoting cooperation. Although she makes it sound like she's hoarding information for the good of the team, she's really putting her needs first.*

Option 5: *This is an incorrect option. You should encourage others to adopt a positive attitude and not complain about taking on unpleasant assignments.*

Summary

Accomplishing team goals and making your team a cohesive unit requires effective communication, mutual trust, and the ability to cooperate. How you approach your work has a great effect on your team's cooperative atmosphere, whether you're a team leader or simply a team member.

By putting the team's needs above your own when the two conflict, you set a cooperative tone. To keep that atmosphere of cooperation, you need to take on all tasks – pleasant and unpleasant – with a positive attitude and avoid any signs of competitiveness.

BUILDING TRUST ON YOUR TEAM

The importance of trust
The three strands that intertwine to make team cohesion can't be separated in actuality. Communication and cooperation depend heavily on the third element – trust. Without trust, a group of people isn't a team; it's just a group of people working in conjunction. These people may communicate and cooperate well, but becoming a cohesive team requires mutual reliance. A team effort means all members must place their chances of success in the hands of the others.

Trust is the confident reliance in the character, abilities, and actions of others. When you trust someone, you believe she will behave in a certain way based on both your personal feelings about her and the available evidence.

So trust has both an emotional and an intellectual component. Your general feelings about someone, your comfort level with the way he behaves, and your intuition about his character all affect your decision to trust.

The emotional component of trust becomes obvious when trust is broken. Few emotions are stronger than the feeling of being betrayed.

The intellectual part of trust involves logically assessing both the situation and the person you're trusting. You decide to trust someone partly based on actual data, such as past actions, past performance, or qualifications. Distrust is a natural reaction to a lack of this sort of information. If you don't know a person or his intentions, and if his way of doing things seems odd or even bizarre to you, you may be reluctant to give him your trust.

Reflect
Have you ever been on a team or in a personal group situation where trust was lacking? Perhaps team members tended to be cynical and aggressive due to prior bad experiences. In what ways did the lack of trust affect team effectiveness?

Costs associated with a lack of trust
On a team without trust, people won't tell one another what they really think. These teams usually just pretend that all is well. Teammates are afraid to take risks. Nobody talks about the real problems for fear of upsetting the status quo. Leaders settle for incremental progress and safe courses of action.

To keep your team from developing a trust-deficient atmosphere, you need to apply strategies for building trust.
But trust can be difficult to achieve in a team situation. To trust someone else, you must relinquish some control of your own destiny, putting control in someone else's hands and making yourself vulnerable.
When you trust, you not only count on your teammates to get the job done, you rely on them to do so in ways you approve of.
This experience of trusting others is what binds team members together. Once trust has been given and shown to be justified, the relationship is strengthened and the sense of belonging to a team is enhanced. Only then will the team be able to have an open exchange of ideas and the freedom to take appropriate risks.
It becomes even harder to trust when you're in a virtual team situation, because trust is based on being able to understand and predict the behavior of your teammates. In a multicultural virtual team, differences in customs, speech, and etiquette – combined with a lack of face-to-face interaction – make trusting all the more challenging.
In any relationship, trust is a vital element that takes time to develop and yet no time at all to lose.

Once lost, trust is difficult to regain. While it may have taken only a single untrustworthy act for trust to disappear, it may take years of trustworthy behavior to regain even a fraction of the former relationship.

Think of the emotionally charged words associated with breach of trust – traitor, deserter, cheat, liar, informant, spy.

Losing your teammates' trust is similar to ruining your credit rating. When you go bankrupt, your credit rating plummets. Regardless of how much money you then manage to earn, your credit rating won't come back up until you've re-established your financial reputation. You must prove yourself trustworthy time and time again to regain some of what you've lost.

Question

Why is trust among team members vital to team cohesiveness?

Options:

1. The experience of trusting binds people together
2. When team members trust each other, there's an open exchange of ideas
3. In an atmosphere of trust, appropriate risks can be taken
4. When teammates act as if they trust each other, more work gets done
5. When team members trust others, they have fewer misunderstandings

Answer

Option 1: *This is a correct option. Giving trust involves opening yourself up and making yourself vulnerable. Finding that your trust was well placed creates an emotional bond to the other person or persons.*

Option 2: *This is a correct option. In an atmosphere of mutual trust, team members aren't afraid to tell the truth, admit mistakes, or look foolish, and ideas can be exchanged freely.*

Option 3: *This is a correct option. When trust is given and received, team members become more willing to take necessary business risks.*

Option 4: *This is an incorrect option. A mere semblance of trust won't increase a team's effectiveness. Trust that's justified and sin-*

cere binds teams together.

Option 5: *This is an incorrect option. Misunderstandings are more likely to result from poor communication.*

Ways to build trust

If trust is such an important and yet fragile thing, how can you build it or regain it when it's been lost? To build trust, the other basic elements for team cohesiveness – good communication and cooperation – need to be present. But then what? Are certain behaviors capable of building trust?

One way of summing up what's needed is the "Be a STAR" method of building trust, which divides the necessary behaviors into four action areas:

- be supportive of your teammates and acknowledge their skills and their contributions
- be truthful when communicating with your fellow team members
- be accountable by taking responsibility for your actions and by sharing responsibility for those of your teammates, and
- be reliable by acting consistently and following through on promises

The S in STAR stands for being **supportive** of your teammates and loyal to your team as a group. When you demonstrate team loyalty, you help create an intimate, friendly, and supportive atmosphere where creativity can flourish and people feel safe being themselves.

To build trust, recognize your teammates' accomplishments and give credit where it's due. Show you value their input and believe them to be competent.

Show you trust your fellow team members by involving them, helping them learn new skills, giving them responsibility, and letting them make decisions for themselves. Team members should never bad-mouth one another behind their backs.

The T in STAR stands for being **truthful**, which applied broadly means you must be trustworthy in your communications. Your teammates know they can rely on you when you say what you mean and mean what you say. They'll share information with you when you're known as someone who gives and receives constructive feedback, admits mistakes, and maintains confidentiality.

The A in STAR represents being **accountable**. Trust grows when team members admit and take responsibility for their mistakes. The point isn't to get down on yourself, but rather take an honest look at what went wrong and move ahead based on what you've learned.

This kind of behavior shows that you're someone who can be relied upon, rather than someone who will try to shift the blame to someone else.

You need to perceive everyone's mistakes, including your own, as team mistakes. Share the responsibility for everyone's actions and address problems together, as a team.

Being accountable sets the tone for communication trust. It creates an environment where team members feel good about taking necessary risks.

Reflect

How does your organization view mistakes? Are teams rewarded for taking reasonable risks? Or are they considered individual problems and punished in some way?

Mistakes and trust

Avoiding all mistakes isn't desirable, as the only way to do this is by shying away from all risk. When mistakes happen, acknowledge them, address them as a team, learn from them, and move on. Team members need to be able to trust that the team will absorb understandable mistakes.

The R in STAR stands for being **reliable**. When trying to build trust on a team, you need to demonstrate to your teammates that they can rely on you to be consistent in matters both large and small.

Predictability builds trust, while unpredictability makes

people nervous. When team members are sure what your response will be, they'll trust you more.
Demonstrate your reliability by following through on commitments and "walking the talk."

Question
The emergency response team at a utilities company is having issues related to lack of trust. People are friendly and encouraging face to face, but some tend to bad-mouth teammates to non-team members behind their backs. One team member has withdrawn and never participates during meetings.
Most members perform pretty well, and Tim, the team lead, does a great job of keeping everyone up to date. He types up the meeting minutes and sends them out in an e-mail within 24 hours of each meeting without fail.
Based on what you know about trust, which behaviors are indicators of a problem with trust?

Options:
1. Some team members bad-mouth teammates to non-team members
2. Tim consistently sends out the meeting minutes
3. A team member has withdrawn and never participates during meetings
4. People are friendly and encouraging

Answer
Behaviors that show a lack of support for teammates indicate a lack of trust. People need to encourage and support each other honestly and be consistent in their actions.

Bad-mouthing teammates and not participating are not the only things to look out for. There are many other indicators of a lack of trust:
failure to show up at meetings
a cynical atmosphere at team meetings people singling out others for blame
an unwillingness to admit mistakes

The financial planning team at a major corporation just completed a series of meetings to resolve next year's budget. Follow along as some of the members discuss the process to learn how team interactions affect the various levels of trust on the team.

Shane: I think we did a great job. We had a ton of good ideas, and Carla's suggestions for reprioritizing the improvements really helped make the whole thing work!

Carla: Thanks, Shane. But it was really a joint effort, except for Margaret. She was so quiet throughout this entire round of meetings. I hardly even noticed she was there. I wonder what her problem is?

Nick: She's probably still feeling a little shy about contributing after the abuse she took when her reorganization project failed so miserably. The boss really let her know that she messed up.

Carla: Yeah, and we could have stopped teasing her about it a little sooner. I think we went a little too far, even though we were only joking. The team's performance has been good overall; so what if we made one little mistake.

Shane: We'll have to let Margaret know that we could really use her input. Maybe if we asked her to take charge of writing the budget summary, she'd know we have confidence in her abilities.

Reflect

Based on your understanding of trust and the "Be a STAR" approach to building it, how would you characterize the finance team's actions? What effects will those actions have on team trust?

The team's actions

Putting Margaret on the spot in the meetings wasn't going to increase her confidence about contributing.

The decision to offer Margaret more responsibility will help rebuild her trust in herself and also the team's trust in her. When trust is lost, only long-term incremental steps will help rebuild it. As Margaret accepts responsibility and successfully completes her tasks, her trust in herself and the trust of her teammates will gradually return.

Question

The environmental sustainability team at an international chemical company is made up of members from five nations. They meet monthly on a conference call.

Which of this virtual team's actions demonstrate strategies for building trust?

Options:

1. Taku asked Martina to help with a particular task and gave her decision-making authority to get the job done.
2. Rather than getting into a discussion about who's to blame for a recent setback, Nils moved the discussion along to how they can catch up.
3. Whenever anyone falls behind, Ayana is ready to set aside what she's doing and help out. She's never said "no."
4. Celeste admits she made a mistake in choosing the financial software and asks for help fixing the problem.
5. The team takes a few minutes at the start of each monthly meeting to summarize the previous month's events.
6. 6. Relationships sometimes get complicated because team members socialize a lot outside of work.

Answer

Option 1: *This is a correct option. You're being supportive and building trust when you involve teammates and give them authority and responsibility.*

Option 2: *This is a correct option. Treating mistakes as team mistakes that require team solutions is part of being accountable. It creates a trust-filled atmosphere in which people feel free to act.*

Option 3: *This is a correct option. Predictability builds trust because the more team members can count on your response, the more they'll trust you.*

Option 4: *This is a correct option. Admitting your mistakes is part of being truthful. This builds trust because people know they can rely on what you say you'll do.*

Option 5: *This is an incorrect option. While it's no doubt a useful action to get everyone "on the same page" for the discussion, summarizing doesn't build trust.*

Option 6: *This is an incorrect option. Although it's good for team members to be familiar, socializing doesn't necessarily build trust.*

Summary

Trust is at the very foundation of team effectiveness. It's vital for a team to have an atmosphere where people feel comfortable taking action, putting forth ideas, and taking the right sort of risks.

Losing your teammates' trust is easy. It can happen with a single untrustworthy act. Building trust, on the other hand, is hard work. And regaining it after it's been lost is even more difficult. One way to build trust on your team is through the "Be a STAR" approach. This method focuses on supporting your teammates, being truthful with them, being accountable for actions as a team, and acting in a consistent way that your teammates can rely on.

IMPROVING TEAM COHESION

Using cohesion-building techniques
Suppose a team is making mistakes and performing poorly. Team spirit is at an all-time low, and relationships among team members are only civil at best. Taking what you've learned about the three main elements of team cohesion, can you pull together the three "strands" of the cord to build the team back up?
Cohesive teams are unified, allowing members to work together in productive harmony. True cohesiveness is only possible when members cooperate with each other, acting together to further the team's goals. Cohesion also requires mutual respect and trust, and it has effective communication at its base.

Suppose you're a manager who's observing the team dynamics of one of your teams. Shirley's team used to be the highest performing team in the company, but lately, the team has been stumbling.
Team morale has been a little low, errors are becoming more common, and the overall energy level of the team seems lower. You wonder if perhaps Shirley's team has a cohesiveness problem. To help determine what's going on, you sit in on team meetings to observe team interactions and the behaviors of team members.
Follow along as team members Hector, Shirley, Charles, and Curt discuss the latest news from upper management.

Shirley: According to the recent department memo, we need to set up a new intranet site for our project. Curt, you're our most experienced web developer. Can we count on you to set up the basic layout?

Curt: Flattery will get you anywhere, Shirley. Sure, I could put the initial pieces together, but Charles is the one who has an eye for design. Charles, would you lend a hand with the basic color scheme?

Charles: Actually, I thought we might have to do this sooner or later, so I have some preliminary designs I've been working on. Just let me know when we can get together.

Curt: Amazing. We can always count on you to be one step ahead. **Hector:** There must be something I could do. I had a great time

working with you two when we designed the last site. **Charles:** Same here!

Hector: Charles, you're way better at this design thing than I would've guessed. Oops, I mean...

Charles: That's alright. I know what you meant. Thanks!

Question
Based on the preceding conversation, is this team showing indicators of problems with cohesiveness?
Options:
1. No
2. Yes
3. Maybe
Answer
Nothing in the conversation so far indicates a cohesiveness issue.

From the previous conversation, it seems like team members are showing signs of good communication. They're also willing to work together as a team and they value each other's skills and abilities. The way Charles reacted to Hector's ambiguous compliment is a pretty good indicator that this is a team that communicates well. Instead of being offended, Charles assumed the

EFFECTIVE TEAMWORK

best intentions and responded positively.

Follow along to continue examining the team members' interactions.

Shirley: So I'll need some volunteers to help me write up the monthly evaluations. How about it? Come on...somebody say something.

Curt: You know I'm no good at that stuff. **Hector:** I'm way too busy.

Shirley: If nobody will volunteer, I'll just have to pick someone.

Charles: Just not me again.

Shirley: Charles, you know you've ducked out of doing this several times. You're going to do it for the team this time. What do you say?

Charles: All right. I guess it'll look good on my resume. **Curt:** That's the spirit! Well...sort of.

Some indicators of poor cooperation came up in the latest discussion between Shirley and her team. Poor cooperation was evident when people tried to avoid writing up the monthly evaluations. Everyone, including Charles, tried to avoid the job in this situation. His actions and his rationale illustrate that he's not putting the team's needs first.

To deal with the cooperation shortage on the team, Shirley, the team lead, encourages Charles to adopt a more collaborative approach, pointing out that what's good for the team is good for him as well. Charles promises to do his best, and from that point on, he tries to remember to accept unwanted tasks with a more positive attitude.

So, Shirley's team communicates well but has some trouble with cooperation. What about the third element – trust? Well, based on their conversations, Shirley's team members don't display any of the common indicators of a lack of trust. Instead, they exchange ideas freely and appreciate each other's skills and contributions.

Question

Here's a chance to practice what you know about team cohesion. Match each problem indicator with the corresponding basic element of cohesion that needs improvement.

Options:
1. After Marcus said to Fiona, "Congratulations on your performance award. It's about time you won one of those," she called him a jerk.
2. Joan said, "I told Isaac I couldn't help him with the advertising mock-ups. I had the time, but it's really not my job."
3. When the team leader asked for opinions about the new change initiative, a hush fell over the meeting.

Targets:
1. Communication
2. Cooperation
3. Trust

Answer

Taking offense and retaliating, as opposed to assuming the best intentions, is a sign of problems with communication.

In a cohesive and cooperative team, members step up and take on tasks with a positive attitude. A "not my job attitude" shows problems with cooperation.

When people withdraw or feel they cannot safely offer opinions, it indicates an environment where trust is lacking.

To increase team cohesion, you must first identify which areas need help based on the various indicators of poor communication, lack of cooperation, and lack of trust. You then apply the appropriate strategies for improving each area.

Case Study: Question 1 of 2

Scenario

For your convenience, the case study is repeated with each question.
Pete's five-person project team has been together for about six months. The members have met previously on earlier projects and get along well on a business level.

Select the names Lee, Sarah, and Karl to learn more about the team's interactions.

Karl

Lately, Karl, a high performer, has been relatively quiet at meetings. Ever since Nina got angry with him for pointing out a mistake she made, he's more careful about phrasing his comments so others won't overreact. In fact, everyone has been a little reluctant to address the real issue, which is overcrowding. The team occupies a single office, and everyone is getting on each other's nerves.

Sarah

Last month, an opportunity for moving the team to a bigger office space was missed because Sarah didn't mention that the space had opened up. She thought the other team members knew about it and they just weren't interested in making the move.

Lee

Lee is typical of most members of the team in that she would never speak poorly of her teammates to anyone outside the group. She's proud of her team, participates fully, and whenever unhealthy competition arises, she makes sure to steer people toward what's good for the team. Like her teammates, she's someone who can be counted on to act consistently and follow through on her commitments.

Question

Which basic team cohesion element is indicated as a problem area?

Options:

1. Cooperation
2. Communication
3. Trust

Answer

Option 1: *This is an incorrect option. The team's ability to get along on a business level*
indicates that members are capable of cooperating. They also show a sense of team loyalty and are conscious of working for the good of the team.

Option 2: *This is the correct option. The indicators – missed opportunities, people being afraid that others will take offense, and failure to deal with underlying issues – all point to a communication problem.*

Option 3: *This is an incorrect option. Trust isn't indicated as a problem when team members can be counted on to act consistently and follow through on commitments, as on this team.*

Case Study: Question 2 of 2

Scenario

For your convenience, the case study is repeated with each question.

Pete's five-person project team has been together for about six months. The members have met previously on earlier projects and get along well on a business level.

Select the names Lee, Sarah, and Karl to learn more about the team's interactions.

Karl

Lately, Karl, a high performer, has been relatively quiet at meetings. Ever since Nina got angry with him for pointing out a mistake she made, he's more careful about phrasing his comments so others won't overreact. In fact, everyone has been a little reluctant to address the real issue, which is overcrowding. The team occupies a single office, and everyone is getting on each other's nerves.

Sarah

Last month, an opportunity for moving the team to a bigger office space was missed because Sarah didn't mention that the space had opened up. She thought the other team members knew about it and they just weren't interested in making the move.

Lee

Lee is typical of most members of the team in that she would never speak poorly of her teammates to anyone outside the group. She's proud of her team, participates fully, and whenever unhealthy competition arises, she makes sure to steer people toward what's good for the team. Like her teammates, she's

EFFECTIVE TEAMWORK

someone who can be counted on to act consistently and follow through on her commitments.

Question

Given the indicators and issue you identified, which actions would you take for building cohesion on this team?

Options:
1. Make sure team members "walk the talk" so that others can learn to rely on their behavior.
2. Get team members to relate on a personal level by providing opportunities to talk informally and get to know one another.
3. Get team members to be more careful about how they respond to ambiguous or negative comments from others.
4. Challenge team members to reduce their space usage. The one who organizes their workspace most efficiently gets Friday afternoons off for a month.
5. Get Sarah to apologize to the team for the missed opportunity.

Answer

Option 1: *This option is incorrect. Being reliable is part of the "Be a STAR" method for building trust, not enhancing communication, which is the problem on Pete's team.*

Option 2: *This option is correct. Providing more opportunities for people to relate on a personal level will help improve overall team communication.*

Option 3: *This is a correct option. When you assume good intentions and choose to move forward in response to ambiguous feedback, you're working toward an environment of open communication.*

Option 4: *This is an incorrect option. Focusing on individual gain in a competition is counterproductive to cooperation and doesn't help communication.*

Option 5: *This is an incorrect option. Pointing the finger at Sarah won't help improve communication, and it may negatively affect cooperation.*

On Pete's team, the indicators pointed to a communication problem. The atmosphere on the team seemed unsafe for honest communication, so opportunities went unmentioned and the real issues weren't addressed. While these issues also bear some relation to trust, the indicators pointed to a communication problem. The solutions you chose needed to address that issue.

Summary

The three main elements of team cohesion – communication, cooperation, and trust – must all be optimally present for a strong team to develop. Various indicators can point to which of the three elements you need to address. By applying strategies targeted at the particular element, you can achieve true unity and cohesiveness, which will in turn take the team to new heights.

EFFECTIVE TEAM COMMUNICATION

Effective communication doesn't just happen. True, some people seem to have an innate ability to always get their points across clearly. And some people seem to be naturally good at listening and getting people to open up. But for many others, perhaps yourself included, effective communication is something they have to work at. And in a team environment, it's vital that you maintain open communication – it's the only way your team can be effective.

Question

How important is effective communication to you? Are you willing to do whatever it takes to ensure your team communicates effectively?

Options:

1. Very willing
2. Somewhat willing
3. Not very willing

Answer

Option 1: *It's great you're very willing to work toward effective communication! You can do many things to enhance your skills – for example, learning how to eliminate verbal communication barriers or how to actively listen to team members. These are both skills you'll learn in this course.*

Option 2: *It's good you're somewhat willing to work toward effective communication. Perhaps if you learn a few strategies for building team communication skills, you'll be more willing to put in the work. This course will give you the information you need to improve your* *communication skills.*

Option 3: *It's too bad you're not very willing to work toward effective team communication. For teams to be effective, they must communicate effectively. Is it possible that you're just unsure of your own ability to communicate effectively? If so, this course will give you the skills you need to eliminate verbal barriers, maintain open communication, and actively listen.*

If you want to enjoy your team experience – and perhaps even become a member of a high-performance team – you'll have to invest some time and effort into building an environment of open, effective communication.

Effective communication requires cooperation between the speaker and the listener.

Without it, frustration levels will rise, misunderstandings will occur, and productivity will decrease.

But don't worry. Even though learning to communicate effectively sounds complicated, it really doesn't have to be. And when you choose to pursue open communication, you and your teammates can enjoy several key benefits. For instance, you'll encourage trust among team members, experience less conflict, increase productivity, and improve the overall cohesiveness of your team.

The first two topics in this course deal with your responsibilities as a speaker. First, you must recognize barriers to effective communication.

Then you can use strategies to remove these barriers.

The third topic deals with your role as a listener, which is to actively listen to your teammates.

Remember, individual team efforts will only get your team so far. Effective and open communication is the fuel that will keep your team going to the finish line.

VERBAL BARRIERS BETWEEN TEAM MEMBERS

Types of verbal barriers
Have you ever been part of a meeting where you couldn't get everyone to understand the point you were trying to make? This can be a frustrating experience. You know that clear communication among team members is vital. But sometimes, interpersonal and communication habits can cause team members to unknowingly establish barriers to effective communication.
Reflect
Think about a time when you had difficulty communicating with your team. What do you think are some reasons you had trouble?
Reasons for communication barriers
Team members sometimes unconsciously sabotage their own effectiveness. This can happen for several reasons:
- they use a lot of technical jargon, which distances people
- they use ambiguous language so others won't know when they're uncertain about something - they block out criticism they don't want to hear from others
- they have a hard time compromising their points of view, which can cause group polarization, and
- they shoot down team members' ideas without considering whether those ideas might work

When people sabotage their own communication efforts, they're using communication barriers. These barriers come in many forms and vary from person to person.

However, all communication barriers reduce productivity and sidetrack teams from their goals.

The first step in eliminating verbal barriers is to recognize them when they occur. Only then can you challenge those barriers and re-establish healthy communication.

You've probably experienced communication barriers, or even used them yourself! When asked to think about a time you had difficulty communicating with your team, you might have listed one or more of the five common types of verbal barriers that hinder effective team performance. These are using jargon, becoming polarized, screening, bluffing, and crushing ideas.

See each type of communication barrier to learn more about it.

Using jargon

People often try to impress others with their use of technical **jargon**, which can include everything from acronyms to technical terms. If it's something that new team members or other stakeholders won't be familiar with, it's jargon.

But this ploy usually backfires because very few people understand what's being said. In fact, it usually makes them feel isolated and keeps them from getting vital information they need. Whenever possible, limit your use of jargon. If you have to use it, be sure to explain your terms. If Mary says "I ran my antivirus program and cleared the cache," she's using jargon.

Becoming polarized

Teams can become **polarized** – broken into opposing groups – when one or more team members can't or won't compromise. When the team is split over an issue, communication between "camps" doesn't flow smoothly. Progress is destroyed, and productivity and morale are diminished.

This often leads to increased levels of team conflict. If your team encounters polarization, defuse it through open discussion. For instance, if Bill asks Mary to back him up in a team dis-

cussion, that's polarizing behavior.
Screening
Does anyone on your team seem to block out constructive criticism from team members, even if they had a valid point? If so, this person is engaging in **screening**. Screening keeps you from feeling hurt, but it also keeps you from learning about things you should change to be a more effective team member.

To counteract this defensive behavior, the team needs a culture of trust. And the person doing the screening must learn to listen to his teammates. If Mary tells Bill that he's being argumentative, and Bill keeps arguing, he's screening.

Bluffing
People often make up responses when asked questions they don't know the answers to. This is called **bluffing** – pretending you know what you're talking about when you don't. What's worse is that people can usually tell when you're bluffing, making you look even more foolish
in the long run!

You may end up giving people incorrect information, which could damage the project. Bluffing destroys your credibility, and people will stop listening to you even when you do know what you're talking about.

So how can you avoid this pitfall? Encourage team members to admit ignorance rather than try to bluff their way through conversations. Do this by modeling the desired behavior. If Mary tells Bill she knows how to install a program on his computer, but really doesn't, she's bluffing.

Crushing ideas
A common communication barrier involves **crushing ideas** – offering automatic and undue criticism of any new idea a team member comes up with. Crushers like to come up with reasons why something won't work instead of figuring out how to make it work. You've probably heard these reasons before – "it'll never work," "it's been done before," and "the boss won't approve it" are all examples of crushing ideas.

This can have a negative effect on team communication, and

you might not always be able to change idea crushers' attitudes. You want team members who are committed to the team and who don't constantly crush the ideas of other people. At the same time, you don't want team members who are easily discouraged by negative comments either.

Suppose Bill brings up an idea for a new product, and Mary tells him that no one would ever buy it. Mary is crushing Bill's idea.

Verbal barriers can hold your team back, and if left unchecked, can eventually destroy it.

Avoiding the defensive behavior of the five types of communication barriers will help your team establish an atmosphere of trust and open communication.

Question

Match each of the verbal barriers to effective communication with its correct definition.

Options:

A. Using jargon
B. Bluffing
C. Becoming polarized
D. Screening
E. Crushing ideas

Targets:

1. Using acronyms and technical terms not familiar to all team members in order to impress people
2. Making up responses when asked questions you don't know the answers to
3. Breaking into opposing groups when one or more team members can't or won't compromise
4. Blocking out constructive criticism from team members, even if they have a valid point
5. Offering automatic and undue criticism of any new idea a team member comes up with

Answer

Using jargon means using acronyms and technical terms not familiar to all team members in order to impress people. This usually makes others feel isolated and keeps them from getting vital information they need.

People often make up responses when asked questions they don't know the answers to. This is called bluffing – pretending you know what you're talking about when you don't.

Teams can become polarized when one or more team members can't or won't compromise. Communication doesn't flow smoothly, progress is destroyed, and productivity and morale are diminished.

Screening is blocking out constructive criticism from team members, even if they have a valid point. Screening keeps you from feeling hurt, but it also keeps you from learning about things you should change to be a more effective team member.

Crushing ideas is offering automatic and undue criticism of any new idea a team member comes up with. Crushers like to come up with reasons why something won't work, instead of figuring out how to make it work.

Recognizing verbal barriers

Now you know what the five types of verbal barriers are, but you also need to be able to recognize them in real-life situations. The best way to learn how to do this is to consider an example.

Ryan, Debbie, Jim, and Sarah are having a team discussion. Follow along and determine if you can identify any communication barriers in the conversation.

Debbie: Jim, I noticed your production figures are down by 5% from last month. It seems like you didn't spend very much time meeting with clients.

Jim: That's not true. I can't believe you think that. And anyway, Ryan didn't get the advertising budget done in time, so I had to wing it when I met with clients.

Jim is defensive.

Ryan: Whoa! Hold on a minute, Jim. I e-mailed you the AM104-B in time for your client meetings. Obviously, you didn't want to use it. Or maybe you just didn't know how?

Ryan is annoyed.

Jim: I would've used that report if it wasn't written in those unintelligible equations you use in all your reports. Why can't you just use plain English and get to the point?

Jim is smug.

Ryan: Those unintelligible equations, as you call them, are used all the time in our field. Everyone on the team should be familiar with them. Sarah, you agree with me, right?

Ryan is defensive.

Sarah: I sure do. I'm surprised you don't understand, Jim. They're used to figure out past sales numbers. You could've asked me for help.

Sarah nods in agreement.

Debbie: Actually, Sarah, the equations are used to project future sales figures. Maybe we should create a document that explains all the difficult terms so we're sure everyone knows them.

Debbie is frustrated.

Sarah: Frankly, I don't see how that'll help. We tried to do something like that a year ago and no one used it then, so why would they now?

Sarah is impatient.

Debbie: I really don't think we're getting anywhere today. Why don't we meet again tomorrow when everyone has had a chance to cool down?

Debbie is starting to get impatient.

Three of the four team members put up communication barriers in the preceding discussion. Can you tell who used jargon inappropriately? Who polarized the team? Who screened input? Who was bluffing? And who was crushing ideas?

See the team members to find out which communication barriers they used.

Jim

Jim screened Debbie's observation that his production figures were down by refusing to acknowledge the comment. Instead, he placed the blame on Ryan.

Ryan

Ryan made his reports incomprehensible by using unnecessary jargon. Then, when confronted with his actions, he polarized the team by asking Sarah to agree with him.
Sarah
Debbie revealed that Sarah was bluffing when she told Jim the equations are for figuring out past sales numbers – she didn't understand the jargon either. Then Sarah crushed Debbie's idea of creating a document to explain the jargon.
Debbie
Debbie was the only team member who didn't use any of the verbal communication barriers.

For a team to be successful, its members must effectively communicate with each other. By recognizing when you or other team members are using verbal communication barriers, you can work at eliminating them.

Question

Match each communication barrier with its related example.

Options:
A. Using jargon
B. Becoming polarized
C. Screening
D. Bluffing
E. Crushing ideas

Targets:
1. "Did you empty the cache before you rebooted?"
2. "I need to get my way on this issue. Will you take my side if I bring it up at the meeting tomorrow?"
3. "I can't believe you think I monopolize meetings. That's not true at all!"
4. "Well of course I understand what you mean by that. It's a method we use to accomplish things."
5. "Who would want to pay in advance for our services? That will never work!"

Answer
Using jargon that others may not understand can lead to miscommunication. Not everyone on your team might understand the term

"cache."

Asking a team member to take your side can lead to the team becoming polarized. This can happen when one or more team members can't or won't compromise.

If a team member is blocking out constructive criticism and becomes defensive by not taking responsibility, that member is screening the input.

Bluffing happens when people make up responses to questions they don't know the answers to. Often, their language is ambiguous, as in "it's a method we use to accomplish things." Your team can avoid this by encouraging members to admit ignorance rather than try to bluff their way through conversations.

Crushing ideas means offering automatic and undue criticism of any new idea a team member comes up with. Telling a team member "That will never work" is a common example of crushing an idea.

Summary

Communication barriers come in many forms and vary from person to person. However, all communication barriers reduce productivity and sidetrack teams from their goals.

In order to eliminate verbal barriers, you first have to recognize them when they occur. Only then can you challenge those barriers and re-establish healthy communication.

The five common types of verbal barriers that hinder effective team performance are using jargon, becoming polarized, screening, bluffing, and crushing ideas.

MAINTAINING OPEN COMMUNICATION ON A TEAM

Strategies for open communication

At one time or another, you've probably found yourself in a meeting with someone who made it difficult for your team to communicate effectively and clearly. It's possible you've even been this person yourself without knowing it! This is actually a common behavior – team members sometimes put up barriers that can hinder effective communication.

You may encounter people who use any of the five typical barriers to effective communication:

some people use jargon or overly technical terminology that not everyone understands some people polarize or divide the team over an issue

some team members screen out constructive feedback from others

some people bluff, pretending they know something when they don't, and

some team members crush the ideas of others without giving them a fair chance

Reflect

What strategies do you use to deal with these barriers to effective communication?

Strategies for open communication

To establish an atmosphere of trust and open communication,

you must create some ground rules that everyone on the team should follow during team meetings, or even during one-on-one discussions. Team members should also use effective anti-barrier strategies to open up communication. These strategies include
- creating a safe environment for team meetings
- getting clarification when you don't understand, and
- maintaining unity on the team

To encourage open communication, you should **create a safe environment for team meetings**. One way to do this is to establish ground rules that ensure discussions are free of criticism and ridicule. People should feel like there are no bad ideas or dumb questions. Team members must have assurance that the meeting is a caring environment, where constructive criticism is given with their welfare in mind.

You can also open up communication by **getting clarification when you don't understand**. Suppose a team member says something that you don't understand, or that you anticipate someone else at the meeting may not follow.

Should you keep quiet to avoid offending the team member? No, you should ask for clarification. You're probably not the only one who's in the dark.

Open communication can be greatly enhanced if you **maintain unity on the team**. Every team has to meet its objectives, solve problems, and make decisions effectively. But this is only possible when all team members pull together and support each other as they carry out their own responsibilities.

If a divisive issue comes up, everyone on the team should search for areas of agreement and resolve conflict as quickly as possible.

The strategies for open communication can all be used during team meetings, but only if everyone remembers to follow them.

The team leader – or whoever facilitates team meetings – should go over these strategies at the first team meeting to ensure that everyone is clear about how meetings will be conducted. Posting the rules on the wall at the beginning of each meeting can also be helpful.

Question

Which strategies can you use to maintain open communication during team meetings?

Options:

1. Create a safe environment for team meetings
2. Get clarification when you don't understand something
3. Maintain team unity
4. Avoid speaking so others don't put down your ideas
5. Give criticism freely without worrying about the recipient's feelings

Answer

Option 1: *This option is correct. To encourage open communication, you should create a safe environment for team meetings. For instance, you could establish ground rules that ensure discussions are free of criticism and ridicule.*

Option 2: *This option is correct. You can open up communication by getting clarification when you don't understand. If a team member says something you don't understand, ask for clarification. You're probably not the only one who's in the dark.*

Option 3: *This option is correct. Open communication can be greatly enhanced if you maintain unity on the team. Teams can only meet their objectives, solve problems, and make decisions effectively when all team members pull together and support each other.*

Option 4: *This option is incorrect. Open communication can only happen when people feel the meeting is a safe environment. Team members should be able to voice their ideas freely without fear of criticism.*

Option 5: *This option is incorrect. To maintain open communication, you should create a safe environment for team meetings. If you give criticism without considering the recipient's feelings, team members won't feel like the meeting is a caring environment.*

Eliminate barriers to communication

You can use each of these strategies – creating a safe environment, getting clarification, and maintaining unity – to remove barriers to effective communication.

For example, when **creating a safe environment for team meetings**, the meeting facilitator should give team members a few principles to follow so they know what to do, and what not to do.

See each guideline to learn what you should and shouldn't do to create a safe environment in team meetings.

What to do

During team meetings, you should treat others the way you'd like to be treated. Think before you speak so your message is clear. And instead of becoming defensive, respond to criticism by using phrases like "I can understand why you might think that" or "I can understand how that could be frustrating for you."

What not to do

Team members will feel safe in meetings if you refrain from snickering, eye-rolling, or whispering to neighbors. Avoid making judgmental criticisms such as "That's the lamest thing I've ever heard."

So how can creating a safe environment for meetings eliminate communication barriers? First, the people who screen out criticism may open up and feel less defensive. They'll be more likely to listen to their team members and change any detrimental behavior.

Bluffing will also decrease, since the insecure members will be assured that nobody on the team is perfect. Knowing others won't ridicule them if they don't know something will reduce the need for them to pretend they have the answers.

Finally, the idea crushers will be silenced, or at least they'll pause and carefully word their criticisms before speaking.

The strategy of **getting clarification when you don't understand** also helps eliminate communication barriers. Don't be afraid to speak up! For instance, if Isaac is using unfamiliar acronyms or technical terms, say "Please explain that in detail." If Mary is talking about a new development as if everyone knows about it, but you don't, speak up and say "Please elaborate." And if Celeste gives an explanation that's confusing or raises your suspicions that she doesn't really understand the issue, ask for clarification.

When team members make it a priority to get clarification when they don't understand, a couple of things will happen.

You'll find that jargon users will learn to stop speaking in code if they're constantly being asked to clarify what they mean.

And bluffing will also decrease. Those "know-it-all" team members will be more honest if they know they'll be asked pointed and clarifying questions about what they say.

The final strategy to help remove barriers to effective communication involves **maintaining unity on the team**. Sometimes teams are divided, and you have to work at bringing them together.

For instance, what if you sense that people are taking sides over an issue, or rallying behind certain team members? In this case, you could try to build bridges between the two sides.

You can also maintain team unity by identifying compromises and win-win solutions. Suppose Margo wants to attend a trade show tomorrow, and Daniel wants the day off. You could say "I know you both have things you want to do tomorrow, but you both can't be out of the office. Margo, why don't you just go to the show in the morning, and Daniel, you can have the afternoon off."

You should also remind team members that a cohesive team is an effective team. Division will hamper good communication and teamwork.

When you maintain unity on the team, you eliminate polarization. People will stop taking sides as they realize that a cohesive team is much more successful than a divided one.

You've learned how to establish open communication in team meetings, but what if you're a member of a virtual team and you don't actually meet face-to-face with your team members? Does that mean you're off the hook from using these ground rules? Not at all. You can apply each of these strategies for maintaining open communication to telephone conversations and e-mail communication, as well as in-person meetings.

Question

If you encountered any of the five barriers to communication, would you know which strategy to apply to eliminate it?

Match the barriers to the strategies. You may use each barrier more than once, and each strategy may receive more than one match.

Options:

A. Using jargon
B. Becoming polarized C. Screening
D. Bluffing
E. Crushing ideas

Targets:

1. Create a safe environment for team meetings
2. Get clarification when you don't understand
3. Maintain unity on the team

Answer

When you create a safe environment for meetings, the screeners will open up and be less defensive, listening to their team members and changing any detrimental behavior. Bluffing will

decrease, since the insecure members will be assured that nobody on the team is perfect. And the idea crushers will be silenced, or at least they'll pause and carefully word their criticisms before speaking.

You'll find that jargon users will stop speaking in code if they're constantly being asked to clarify what they mean. And bluffers will be more honest if they know they'll be asked pointed and clarifying questions about what they say.

When you maintain unity on the team, you eliminate polarization. People will stop taking sides as they realize that a cohesive team is much more successful than a divided one.

Ground rules for open communication

EFFECTIVE TEAMWORK

During your meeting with Judy, Bob, Melissa, Chris, and Carol, team members demonstrated several communication barriers. If you applied the strategies for creating a safe environment, getting clarification, and unifying the team, you helped eliminate the use of these barriers and came to a resolution.

Summary

The five typical barriers to effective communication are using jargon, becoming polarized, screening, bluffing, and crushing ideas.

To create an atmosphere of trust and open communication, you need to establish ground rules that everyone on the team should follow during team meetings. Team members should also use the following anti-barrier strategies to open up communication: create a safe environment for team meetings, get clarification when you don't understand, and maintain unity on the team.

ACTIVELY LISTENING TO TEAM MEMBERS

The importance of active listening

Marty is a new leader who's been hearing rumblings of discontent among his team members. His own boss told him that several employees have mentioned they find Marty difficult to talk to and pointed to how he doesn't seem interested in what they have to say. People are afraid to speak up because they think he's overly critical of their ideas. Marty wants to be a good leader, but he can't figure out why there's friction between himself and his team members. Can you figure out Marty's problem?

If you said that Marty isn't a good listener, you're right. Many leaders don't have a clue how to improve their listening skills, and this is unfortunate. Being a good listener is vital to effective team communication.

When you're with teammates, you should practice active listening. This simply means that you actively take in what the speaker is saying, but you don't add input of your own.

In active listening, you encourage the speaker to continue talking and to clarify what he's saying. It's a speaker-centered process, and it gives the speaker implicit permission to continue talking.

Question
How would you assess your own ability as an active listener?
Options:
1. I sometimes interrupt the speaker.
2. I listen silently while the other person is speaking.

3. I use both verbal and nonverbal cues to show I'm listening.
Answer

Option 1: *If you tend to interrupt people while they're speaking, you're not actively listening to them. What you should do instead is let the person finish talking, and then ask questions or reflect on what he has said. Don't worry – you'll learn more about these techniques in this topic.*

Option 2: *Listening silently while someone is speaking is definitely preferable to interrupting!*

But an even better way to show you're actively listening is to give verbal cues, such as nodding encouragingly, while the speaker is talking. You'll learn more about this technique – reflecting – and others in this topic.

Option 3: *Empathizing and using verbal and nonverbal cues are great ways to show the speaker that you're actively listening! It sounds like you're a good listener already, but taking this topic may provide you with more techniques you can use to improve your listening skills further.*

When you actively listen to your team members, rather than merely hearing the words they're speaking, you'll find there are several benefits of active listening. For one thing, when people can talk freely, you'll be better able to identify problem areas that might exist on a project. Another benefit of active listening is that you can prepare better negotiation and conflict management strategies, as well as make decisions based on the information you draw out in a conversation.

When you actively listen, you'll be able to:
- *Identify problem areas*
- *Prepare better negotiation and conflict management strategies*
- *Make decisions based on information from conversation*

When you actively listen, you'll also be in a better position to resolve problems among clients, project team members, and other stakeholders. That's because supportive behavior is more conducive to cohesive teams.

And finally, active participation from team members leads to more innovation and creativity. When people ask questions, be supportive while you're listening – you may find that ideas begin to flow more freely.

Remember, the difference between listening and hearing is that hearing is a passive process – in a way, it only requires ears and a brain.

Question

Why is active listening important to healthy team communication?

Options:
1. You'll be able to identify problem areas on projects
2. You can prepare better negotiation and conflict management strategies
3. You'll be more effective at resolving problems
4. You'll be able to discourage team members who just like to hear themselves talk
5. You can ensure that you're the only one whose ideas get heard

Answer

Option 1: *This option is correct. When people can talk freely, you'll be better able to identify problem areas that might exist on a project.*

Option 2: *This option is correct. One benefit of active listening is that you can prepare better negotiation and conflict management strategies, as well as make decisions based on the information you draw out in a conversation.*

Option 3: *This option is correct. When you actively listen, you'll be in a better position to resolve problems among clients, project team members, and other stakeholders because supportive behavior is conducive to cohesive teams.*

Option 4: *This option is incorrect. The goal of active listening is to encourage team members to engage and actively participate in team conversations. When people ask questions, be supportive while you're listening.*

Option 5: *This option is incorrect. When you try to be the only person whose ideas get heard, you're not actively listening to team mem-*

bers. Instead, when you're with teammates, practice active listening and take in what the speaker is saying.

Techniques for active listening
Reflect
Think about the way you listen to people, especially when you're practicing active listening. Are there any specific techniques you use?

Techniques for active listening
Your list may have included some of the four techniques that are commonly used for active listening: inquiring, acknowledging, reflecting, and suspending judgment.

Members of your team will feel valued when it's clear you're listening to them. And one way to show them you're listening is by using such techniques as inquiring, acknowledging, reflecting, and suspending judgment. For example, you might ask an open-ended query to invite a team member to speak. Open-ended queries require more than a "yes" or "no" answer. The goal of **inquiring** like this is to invite your teammate to begin speaking by asking something like "What do you think?" or "How do you feel about that?"

Asking open-ended questions sounds pretty straightforward, doesn't it? And sometimes, it is, but other times, it isn't.

If a teammate is excited or upset about something, that person is going to expect you to respond appropriately – to be sensitive to his emotional state.

If a team member is happy, be happy with him. If the person is upset, respond neutrally so you don't feed the fire. Also, if someone's demeanor makes it obvious how he feels, don't ask, "How do you feel about that?"

Remember Marty from earlier in this topic? He's a new leader who can't understand why his team members seem unhappy with his leadership. Follow along as Marty uses the inquiring technique as he talks with Jodie, one of his team members.

Marty: Jodie, I really appreciate that you're willing to talk with me.

Jodie: Sure Marty, no problem.

Marty: I've heard through the grapevine that some team members think I'm hard to talk to. Can you shed some light on that? **Jodie:** Well...are you sure you won't be offended?

Jodie is hesitant.

Marty: Not at all. I really need to know. *Marty is encouraging.*

Jodie: OK, here's the deal. Sometimes you're very abrupt when someone asks you a question. It's almost like you have better things to be doing.

Marty: Oh no! I want everyone to feel like they can ask me questions. I really need to work on that. Is there anything else you can think of?

Marty is embarrassed.

Jodie: Actually, there is. Remember the other day when I brought up my idea for a new product? I felt like you shot me down without even hearing what I was saying.

Marty: Wow, I'm sorry Jodie. That wasn't my intent. The thing is, one of our competitors just released a similar product. I guess I should've made that clear.

Marty is apologetic.

Jodie: Yeah, that would have been good to know. **Marty:** Well, thanks for being honest!

When Marty spoke with Jodie, he could have easily asked closed-ended questions such as "Do you think I'm a good listener?"

Instead, he asked open-ended questions to get specific answers. By using the inquiring technique, Marty found out exactly why he wasn't connecting with team members.

Another technique for active listening is **acknowledging**. When you acknowledge teammates effectively, you're showing them that you're listening and open to hearing what they have to say.

Question

Which do you think are ways to acknowledge a speaker?

Options:
1. Give short verbal responses
2. Use nonverbal body language
3. Change the expression on your face
4. Stop the speaker to ask a question
5. Maintain a still and calm demeanor

Answer

To acknowledge a speaker, you should give short verbal responses, use nonverbal body language, and change your facial expressions.

Verbal acknowledgment consists of saying things like "Yes," "I see," or "Uh-huh."

And just as with the technique of inquiring, you need to be sensitive to your teammate's emotional state in order to respond appropriately.

Nonverbal cues to show that you're listening include nodding your head, making eye contact, and leaning toward the speaker slightly.

Follow along as Marty uses the acknowledging technique as he continues his discussion with Jodie.

Marty: You've given me a lot to think about. What would you say I could do to improve my relationship with you and the rest of the team?

Marty is sincere.

Jodie: Well, for one thing, you need to make people feel like you're interested in what they have to say. That would make a big difference.

Jodie is being honest.

Marty: Right, right. *Marty agrees.*

Jodie: And stop being so critical! At least, try to make us feel like you appreciate our ideas, even if you don't think they're good.

Jodie continues to be honest.

Marty: Uh-huh. Good point. *Marty agrees.*

Jodie: One other thing. Try being more approachable. Act like a team member instead of a scary boss.

Jodie advises.

Marty: I see. Those are good points, Jodie. Again, I appreciate your honesty.

Marty is pleased.

Did you notice how Marty acknowledged Jodie's comments without defending himself? This showed that he was listening and open to her suggestions.

Another active listening technique is **reflecting**, which involves paraphrasing or repeating what the speaker has said. You might start off with phrases like "So you're saying..." or "You seem to think that..." Then restate the big issue – not just one part of what was said. When someone is upset about something, this isn't only a good way to be a supportive listener, it also helps defuse the emotion. If you focus on only a part of the whole, the speaker could become more agitated or just irritated that you weren't listening after all.

After his discussion with Jodie, Marty goes to speak with his boss, Nathan. Follow along as they have a conversation.

Marty: I was just talking to Jodie, and I think I've figured out why the team hasn't warmed up to me. I want to talk to you to find out if you have any other suggestions for me.

Nathan: I'm glad you brought that up, Marty. In two weeks, there's a course being offered on effective communication. I think you would really benefit from attending.

Marty: So you think I could improve my relationship with my team members by taking the course?

Nathan: Absolutely! **Marty:** Great, sign me up!

When Nathan told Marty that taking the communication course would be beneficial, Marty practiced reflecting by paraphrasing what Nathan said.

The final technique for active listening is **suspending judgment**, and it can be one of the most difficult to put into practice. What exactly does it mean to suspend judgment? Well, when you're having a conversation, stop arguing in your head with the speaker when you're supposed to be listening.

When you're too busy creating a reply in your head, or analyzing what the speaker is saying, you're not listening! And if you're running through a list of reasons why an idea won't work or why the speaker is wrong, guess what? That's not listening either.

Remember Marty's earlier conversations with Jodie? He seemed very understanding about her criticism and took it on board. But Marty could have been thinking about other things while Jodie spoke.

See each of Jodie's statements to find out what kind of thoughts Marty needed to suspend while Jodie was speaking.

Jodie said "Sometimes you're very abrupt when someone asks you a question," and Marty responded "Oh no! I want everyone to feel like they can ask me questions." Then Jodie said "I felt like you shot me down without even hearing what I was saying," to which Marty responded "Wow, I'm sorry Jodie. That wasn't my intent." Finally, Jodie said "You need to make people feel like you're interested in what they have to say" and Marty agreed by saying "Right, right."

Jodie said "Sometimes you're very abrupt when someone asks you a question," and Marty responded "Oh no! I want everyone to feel like they can ask me questions."

Marty welcomed Jodie's feedback, but he struggled with a thought when Jodie mentioned he was abrupt when people asked him questions. He was thinking "That's because I don't have time for questions from people with less experience than I have."

Jodie said "I felt like you shot me down without even hearing what I was saying," to which Marty responded "Wow, I'm sorry Jodie. That wasn't my intent."

Although Marty was apologizing to Jodie, in his head, he realized he was leaping to conclusions as he thought "And you probably felt like I was ignoring you, didn't you?"

Jodie said "You need to make people feel like you're interested in what they have to say" and Marty agreed by saying "Right, right."

Marty acknowledged Jodie's comment verbally, but in his head, he realized he was analyzing her words as he thought "Do people really think that about me? That's crazy. I always act like I'm interested!"

Question

Larry and Bart are team members. Larry has just received a warning from his supervisor, and Bart is letting him blow off steam.

Which are examples of Bart using the different techniques to actively listen to his teammate's viewpoint?

Options:
1. Bart responds to Larry by saying "From what you just said, it sounds like you're feeling pretty frustrated and stuck."
2. As Larry is talking, Bart becomes aware that he's thinking to himself "Hey, our company policy forbids managers from giving warnings without documentation!"
3. Bart says to Larry, "So Larry, what do you think you're going to do now?"
4. As Larry is speaking, Bart encourages him by occasionally nodding his head and saying "Really?"
5. When Larry explains his frustration, Bart says "So how do you feel about that, Larry?"

Answer

Option 1: *This option is correct. Bart is practicing reflection by paraphrasing what Larry has just said.*

Option 2: *This option is correct. By realizing that he's thinking when he should be listening to Larry, Bart is practicing suspending judgment.*

Option 3: *This option is correct. Bart is asking Larry an open-ended question, which will invite him to speak – Bart is practicing inquiring.*

Option 4: *This option is correct. Bart is practicing acknowledging, which involves using verbal and nonverbal cues to show Larry he's listening and open to hearing what he has to say.*

Option 5: *This option is incorrect. If a teammate is upset about something, you need to respond appropriately. Larry's demeanor makes it pretty obvious that he's upset, so Bart shouldn't ask "How do you feel about that?"*

Summary

When you're with teammates, you should practice active listening. This involves actively taking in what the speaker is saying without adding your own input.

Active listening has several benefits. You'll be able to identify problem areas on projects, as well as prepare better negotiation and conflict management strategies. And you'll also be more effective at resolving problems.

You can use four common techniques for actively listening: inquiring, acknowledging, reflecting, and suspending judgment. Taking the time and effort to use these techniques will help build solid team relationships.

USING FEEDBACK TO IMPROVE TEAM PERFORMANCE

Perhaps you've heard the proverb "See no evil, hear no evil, speak no evil." While its origin and meaning are still debated, one common, modern interpretation is that it describes the desire to avoid becoming involved in a situation. Imagine how your team would function if all its members shared this philosophy.

Most business experts would agree that if you have information and ideas that would help someone perform better, it's practically unethical not to share them. This is strong, yet appropriate, advice for teams that want to achieve optimal performance.

Members of effective, high-performing teams communicate assertively, and regularly give and receive constructive feedback. Seeing nothing, hearing nothing, and saying nothing won't work if your team wants to achieve optimal performance.

Typically, high-performing teams use feedback to recognize desired performance and to provide guidance on how to improve performance. Feedback is also commonly used to help solve problems, clarify expectations, keep team members moving toward the same goals, and show appreciation.

And as a team member, you're responsible for giving constructive feedback when you can, and receiving feedback graciously when it's offered.

The key to your ability to give and receive feedback is your interpersonal skills. As you learn to give and receive feedback, you'll likely experience some personal growth.

Teams will grow too. A team whose members trust each other's intentions and treat one another with respect will exchange feedback more effectively. Members will be more confident about contributing and supporting each other on performance-related matters.

This effort provides beneficial side effects, including improvements in productivity, morale, and job satisfaction. All of this helps enhance team performance and enrich the team environment.

This course covers the two aspects of feedback. See each aspect to learn more.

Giving constructive feedback
In the first lesson, you'll learn about the importance of assertive communication to the success of high-performing teams. You'll also get to practice principles that will help you give appropriate and effective feedback.

Receiving feedback graciously
In the second lesson, you'll learn how to receive feedback graciously.

Upon completion of this course, you'll be able to use techniques for giving and receiving feedback to your advantage.

PRINCIPLES FOR GIVING FEEDBACK ON A TEAM

Being assertive

"You did this wrong, again!" Have you ever heard this or something similar at work? You probably agree that it's not very useful feedback.

As a member of a team, you need feedback on your performance so you can improve. Effective teams share feedback on what is and what isn't working, with the end goal being optimal performance.

And why is this type of feedback important? Because the performance of individual team members impacts team performance, and team performance impacts the organization's performance. So, in some respects, the optimal performance of your organization as a whole starts with you and your ability to give constructive feedback to a fellow team member.

First, you need to know when to give feedback. Watch for these signs. They indicate that feedback is required:
- a strong performer's work is slipping
- behavior is negatively impacting the team
- known issues or concerns remain unresolved, and
- errors occur repeatedly

Question
Now that you have an appreciation for the importance of feedback, how would you rate your ability to share feedback?

Options:
1. Excellent
2. Good
3. Poor

Answer

Option 1: *You indicated that your ability to share feedback is excellent. The advice given in this topic may offer new information that will further improve the ease with which you give feedback and the effectiveness of your feedback.*

Option 2: *You indicated that your ability to share feedback is good. Improving your ability to give feedback by learning ways to give it effectively will improve your comfort level with giving feedback.*

Option 3: *You indicated that your ability to share feedback is poor. Giving feedback can be tricky, and if you're hesitant, that's understandable. Learning how to effectively give feedback will help you become more comfortable and confident when the need arises.*

Teams made up of assertive communicators are generally more successful. However, two other typical communication styles are common and should be discouraged – passive and aggressive. Assertive communication strikes a balance between these two styles.

Like other forms of communication, feedback needs to be assertive.

What does it mean to be assertive? People who use this style of communication believe they're entitled to express their ideas, needs, and opinions. They take responsibility for their feelings and actions, while respecting the needs and dignity of others.

Assertive communication helps to build trust and credibility, which, in a team environment, can enhance productivity and effectiveness. Assertiveness is the essential characteristic for effective team communication.

Assertive feedback is direct, honest, and respectful of the rights, needs, feelings, and dignity of others. Using this approach to deliver feedback makes it possible to express feelings and unpleasant news in a manner that others can accept without becoming defensive. As such, assertive communication promotes productivity, improvement, and team harmony.

Here is an example of assertive feedback: "I noticed in the article you just submitted that you failed to apply house style guidelines for the use of acronyms. Can you review the guidelines and apply them next time?"

Passive feedback is generally apologetic and unclear. The absence of self-confidence and self-respect on the part of the giver results in feedback that lacks clarity, conviction, and confidence.

Receivers are generally left confused about the intended message and what's expected of them. The impact on performance will probably be negligible.

For example, "I've just reviewed your article. While I suspect you've done a better job than I would have, you may want to watch your use of house style."

Aggressive feedback tends to be confrontational and hostile, which tends to put the receiver on the defensive. You'll know aggressive feedback by the demands made of, or the pressure placed on, the receiver. You may even hear some cursing or screaming. Essentially, the lack of respect for others and the win-at-all-costs approach that drives aggressive feedback has a negative impact on the team.

For example, "I noticed you decided not to use house style. All of your acronyms were done wrong. What a waste of my time!"

Tim and Darryl are welders for a heavy construction team. Tim is cutting steel beams, and Darryl has noticed the cuts are repeatedly inaccurate, wasting time and resources. Follow along for examples of ways Darryl might approach Tim.

Passive: Tim, can I speak to you? The precision of your cuts is terrific, but your measurements are off. Maybe there's a problem with the blade?

Darryl says with a worried look.

Assertive: Tim, I've noticed you're not consistent with your cuts. Would you take additional effort to make sure your cuts are exact?

Darryl says with a smile.

Aggressive: Tim, what are you doing? Do you have any idea how much your cutting errors are affecting our schedule, not to mention the wasted materials and effort?

Darryl says angrily.

In the preceding scenario, Darryl approached Tim in three different ways: passively, assertively, and aggressively. Tim's attitude and reaction to Darryl would be dependent on which approach Darryl took. Clearly, the most effective approach was being assertive. It will work for you too.

Question

A project team is working to develop a new repellant for a pest that threatens to devastate old-growth forests. Julie has noticed that Geoff has forgotten to enter important data during his recent visual inspection of a test population. She needs to say something to Geoff, since continued omissions such as this can render the experiment ineffective.

Select the statement in which Julie is communicating assertively.

Options:
1. "I noticed you didn't enter any data, but it's important you complete this, otherwise the experiment will be useless."
2. "Geoff, why didn't you write down your observation? Are you trying to ruin my work?"
3. "I noticed that the observations for the last inspection weren't recorded. I sure hope that doesn't hurt our results too much. I hate to mention it, but could you be more careful next time?"

Answer

Option 1: *This option is correct. Julie has been assertive. She has expressed her need in a direct and respectful manner.*

Option 2: *This option is incorrect. This is an example of aggressive communication. It's rather confrontational and is likely to provoke a defensive response from Geoff.*

Option 3: *This option is incorrect. Julie isn't clearly expressing herself. This is a passive response that may fail to resolve the problem.*

Giving effective feedback

Feedback should be communicated assertively, but how do you deliver it? Giving effective feedback can be tricky. What you say, when you say it, and how you say it can impact the effectiveness of your message.

In addition to being assertive, feedback must follow four more principles to be effective:
- it must be specific
- it must be descriptive
- it must be given in the right setting, and
- it must be given in a timely fashion

The first principle, **specific**, means your feedback should be factual and relate directly to the action or behavior you're commenting on. Avoid being vague or introducing hearsay. By being factual and specific, your message will be clear, and you'll reduce the chances the receiver will overreact or become defensive.

For example, suppose a coworker did something that you believe to be inappropriate. In response, you give this feedback: "In our meeting this morning, you laughed when I asked about the environmental implications of the development."

You have clearly and specifically identified the behavior and incident you're referring to, and have refrained from commenting beyond the facts.

Question
Which is a good example of a specific opening sentence for feedback?
Options:
1. "John, I've noticed you've been late twice this week." 2. "John, you really need to get your act together."
3. "John, I hear you've been late several times recently."
Answer

Option 1: *This is the correct option. This opening sentence defines the specific behavior, and the receiver will clearly understand what you're referring to.*
Option 2: *This option is incorrect. This statement is too vague, and John can't know for sure what behavior or action has prompted your comment.*
Option 3: *This option is incorrect. Specific feedback needs to be observable, and this statement is based on hearsay. It's also not factual – what does "several times recently" actually mean? John could interpret your statement in various ways.*

The next principle to apply when giving feedback is to be **descriptive** rather than judgmental. Base your feedback on observable behavior. Don't cloud the truth with judgments about your team member's attributes or assumptions about why the person did what she did. This serves no useful purpose and can incite anger or defensiveness in the receiver.

Compare these examples of descriptive and judgmental feedback:
- "You were 20 minutes late" is descriptive, while "You have poor management skills" is judgmental.
- "This report doesn't meet our formatting standards" is descriptive, but "You're sloppy and don't pay attention to standards" is judgmental.

Question
As part of a project team, you're responsible for collating progress briefs for a report for the board of directors. You've just noticed that one of your colleagues, Omar, hasn't submitted a brief yet, and it was supposed to be in yesterday. You need it by the end of the day to get the report ready for the board.
What should you say to Omar?
Options:
1. "Omar, I notice you haven't yet submitted your progress brief for the project, and I need it to submit to the board."

2. "Omar, where's your brief? I guess all the stress you're under is getting to you, huh?"
3. "Omar, I need your work by the end of the day."
4. "Omar, I need your progress brief."

Answer

Option 1: *This is the correct option. You've clearly specified which report you're speaking of and have described the situation without making any judgments.*

Option 2: *This option is incorrect. You haven't specified which brief you're talking about, and you've made assumptions as to why Omar hasn't submitted his work.*

Option 3: *This option is incorrect. This statement is too vague. Omar probably has a hefty workload and may not understand what you're talking about.*

Option 4: *This option is incorrect. This is more of a request than feedback. You haven't been specific or descriptive. Omar won't necessarily understand your point.*

The next principle to apply when giving feedback is to choose an appropriate **setting**. As a general rule, feedback should be given in private. Feedback given in private tends to be more effective because the receiver is likely to be more relaxed, focused, and open when others are out of earshot.

Find a private setting where nobody will overhear you or walk in on you, such as an office or meeting room. Common areas such as a cubicle, the water cooler, or the lunchroom are inappropriate places to give feedback. Delivering feedback in private is especially important when the feedback could embarrass the receiver.

However, sometimes public feedback is appropriate. For example, when a group feedback forum has been established, and team members are accustomed to receiving feedback publicly.

The final principle you should follow when giving feedback is to give it in a **timely** fashion. Give it as soon as possible after the action or behavior requiring feedback occurs.

Promptly giving feedback has a couple of advantages. See each advantage for more information.

Keeps incident fresh in mind
One advantage to promptly giving feedback is that it keeps the incident fresh in both the giver's and receiver's mind.

Feedback better received
When you give feedback right away, it's likely to be better received. A time lapse between when an incident happens and when feedback is given can make the receiver feel uncomfortable. She may wonder why you waited so long to tell her she wasn't performing satisfactorily. Or she may not recall the incident. Either way, the feedback will be less effective and runs the risk of damaging relationships and not enhancing performance.

Question
Recall the example where your colleague, Omar, hadn't submitted a brief on time. Well, take a step back.
Before you deliver the feedback, which action demonstrates the most effective use of the principles of choosing a setting and being timely?
Options:
1. You ask Omar to join you in a meeting room as soon as you realize you don't have his brief
2. You find Omar in the lunchroom and demand the brief be on your desk in ten minutes
3. You submit the progress report without Omar's brief and send an e-mail to all team members reminding them to get their work in on time
4. You submit the progress report without Omar's brief, but you ask him to come see you when he gets a chance

Answer
Option 1: *This option is correct. Asking Omar to join you in a meeting room is the most appropriate action to take. You've met in private, and you've done so in a timely manner. Now, Omar might be able to complete his work in time to include it in the report, which is in the best interest of the entire team.*

Option 2: *This option is incorrect. Searching for Omar and discussing the issue wherever you find him isn't appropriate. Your discussion should happen in private.*

Option 3: *This option is incorrect. Submitting the progress report without first talking to Omar isn't very productive. Given a chance to respond, Omar may have been able to get the brief to you in time.*

Option 4: *This option is incorrect. Asking Omar to come see you when he gets a chance won't help get the brief in the report on time. And when you do give Omar the feedback, he may resent the fact you didn't give it right away.*

Summary

The ability to give feedback appropriately is essential to building and maintaining a high-performance team. When all team members share feedback, team performance improves. And improved team performance means better overall performance.

Effective feedback is assertive, specific, descriptive, and given in private, in a timely fashion.

PRACTICE GIVING FEEDBACK AS A MEMBER OF A TEAM

Giving feedback

As a member of a team, you need to be able to give feedback. Practice applying the principles of appropriate feedback in a realistic RolePlay. As you work through the RolePlay, keep in mind that effective feedback is assertive, specific, descriptive, given in private, and given in a timely fashion.

Assume you own a massage therapy clinic and are a partner in an association that collectively offers nutrition, massage therapy, and fitness services at a local health club. Recently, the health club lost a prominent personal trainer. You know the fallout has been difficult, and the club is scrambling to fill the void left by the departed trainer.

One of your clients has just complained that she's been waiting for over a month for a follow-up consultation with another trainer, Lee.

You fear that the chaos in the club will negatively impact all the businesses in the association. So, you decide to discuss this matter with Lee, the trainer involved in the complaint you've just heard.

Question
How should you approach Lee?
Select the statement that demonstrates the most appropriate time and place to talk to Lee.

Options:

1. Approach Lee privately and tell him you've just heard something that you'd like to talk about in the meeting room as soon as possible
2. Interrupt Lee while he's speaking to a client and tell him you've just heard a complaint from a fitness club client that concerns you
3. Approach Lee the next time you see him, and tell him you'd like to talk to him in private about something you heard a while back

Answer

Option 1: *This is the correct option. Asking Lee to meet privately to discuss something you've just heard demonstrates that you're being timely and have chosen an appropriate setting for the discussion.*

Option 2: *This option is incorrect. While you're applying the principle of dealing with the issue in a timely fashion, it's inappropriate to interrupt Lee in front of his client.*

Option 3: *This option is incorrect. You're right to ask to speak to Lee in private, but it sounds like you've waited too long. Feedback should be given as soon as possible following the incident that requires attention.*

Summary

Always communicate assertively, and be specific and descriptive when giving feedback. This will help you communicate more clearly.

And remember, delivering feedback in private helps ensure the receiver can concentrate on what you're saying.

Finally, give your feedback as soon as possible. Because people tend to forget details, the more time that passes, the more awkward and potentially ineffective your feedback will be.

STRATEGIES FOR RECEIVING FEEDBACK FROM TEAM MEMBERS

Benefits of receiving feedback

Have you ever made the observation about a colleague that "he can dish it out, but he sure can't take it?" How receptive are you to "taking it?" Feedback is valuable information – even when it's unpleasant – but what you choose to do with it is up to you.

Most of us have received feedback at one time or another. And generally speaking, we all react in one of two ways. Select each typical reaction to learn how it impacts feedback.

Graciously

Receiving feedback graciously means listening courteously with an open mind for the truth in the feedback. This also means moving forward with a positive attitude, and learning from and applying the feedback in an effort to improve and grow.

Defensively

Receiving feedback defensively means letting your ego get in the way or letting your pride be hurt. The typical reaction is that you argue back at the person. This can lead to resentment – you learn nothing this way, and you don't grow or change as a result of the feedback.

Even if you manage to receive feedback graciously, you should still take a closer look at all feedback you receive. This can help you to process the information. You may want to start by asking yourself "Was it justified? Was it fair?"

Next, consider the source of the feedback. Begin by considering what you know about the person giving the feedback. Can you trust this person? What about the person's intentions – are they clear? What was the person's demeanor while expressing the feedback? Calm or upset? Is this person qualified to offer the feedback?

What about the circumstances that brought about the feedback? Did the behavior or action that prompted the feedback stem from unusual circumstances? Was it something you had control over? What are the consequences of the action or behavior?

The greatest benefit of constructive feedback is its value as a means of improving performance. Always take the time to learn from and apply any feedback you receive. This is especially important if it came from a reliable source and the circumstances indicate that you may not have been behaving correctly.

Question

So by learning to graciously accept constructive feedback, you may realize a benefit – that your own performance improves. What other benefits do you think might come from learning to accept constructive feedback graciously?

Options:
1. Encourages personal growth
2. Builds respect
3. Provides an opportunity to build role models 4. Ensures that all feedback is constructive
5. Separates the leaders from the followers

Answer

Option 1: *This option is correct. Receiving feedback can be difficult. Accepting feedback graciously may require you to grow personally*

– to develop better communication and interpersonal skills. It also rewards the person who had the courage to deliver the feedback in the first place, by offering her a chance to grow personally from the experience.

Option 2: This option is correct. Graciously receiving feedback requires humility and approachability. When team members establish a reputation for being humble and approachable, they gain the respect of other members of the team. This is beneficial because team relationships built on respect are the most successful kind.

Option 3: This option is correct. Team members who can receive feedback graciously become role models for other members of the team. This can help to build a high-performing team, and high-performance teams use feedback to more effectively and efficiently achieve their goals.

Option 4: This option is incorrect. Not all feedback will be constructive. The person giving the feedback may have ulterior motives or isn't qualified to offer feedback. This is why it's important to consider the source of feedback.

Option 5: This option is incorrect. Graciously receiving feedback is something all team members must be able to do.

Graciously receiving feedback

A simple process can help you receive feedback graciously. Now, you'll learn to use this process as a way to graciously receive feedback. The elements of the process are listening, clarifying, and acknowledging.

The first two elements – listening and clarifying – are iterative. You'll likely practice these over and over again, as appropriate, during the process of receiving feedback.

Effective listening is the key to receiving feedback. Here are several techniques that can help you learn to listen effectively: listen without interrupting, avoid negative thoughts, and signal that you're listening.

When someone is giving you feedback, listen without interrupting. Allow the speaker to complete her train of thought and say all she has to say. Don't even interrupt to get clarification.

This helps you and the person giving the feedback to remain focused.

As you listen, use receptive language to signal you're listening. Phrases such as "I see" and "uh-huh" let the speaker know you're listening and following the conversation. It also encourages the speaker to continue and helps you remain focused on what's being said. Avoid words or phrases that simply imply a response is required, as they can derail the feedback as the speaker stops to address your concern.

Avoid negative thoughts. It's quite natural that as we process information, we react to it. If you notice your thoughts are negative, try to stop thinking that way. It's hard to listen and remain focused when you're formulating arguments or judging what's being said. The key here is to remain open-minded. You'll avoid potential misunderstandings if you delay your reaction and response until the person is finished explaining herself.

Sam, an architect, and Hilary, a graphic designer, are working together on a project. Hilary created a computer-generated architectural model of a proposed water treatment facility for Sam to use in his meeting with the project stakeholders. Sam has just finished reviewing the model and has some feedback for Hilary. Follow along as Hilary receives Sam's feedback.

Sam: Hilary, your rendering of the proposed facility is excellent. I think a couple of improvements would increase the effectiveness of the animation.

Hilary: Right...

Hilary is actively listening.

Sam: First, I'd like you to slow down the opening animation. Currently, a 360 degree view is given, and I found this a bit disorienting. I think it would be more effective if the animation switched between the four exposures.

Hilary: Uh-huh...

Hilary maintains her interest.

Sam: And pausing momentarily at each one would give viewers a chance to orient themselves. Try adding some geographic landmarks, like trees or buildings that would be seen in the

background from the different views – that sort of thing.
Hilary: OK...
Hilary continues to listen intently to Sam's feedback.
Sam: Also, consider adding a compass that will change to indicate the elevation as the view switches.

Question
At first, Hilary did find it hard to accept the feedback and realized she was judging the information. But she quieted her negative thoughts and chose instead to keep an open mind and focus on what Sam was saying.
Hilary did some other things right too. What were they?
Options:
1. Listened without interrupting
2. Used receptive language
3. Considered the source
4. Formulated a good excuse for her work

Answer
Option 1: *This option is correct. Hilary didn't interrupt Sam as he was talking. Sam was able to express himself without being sidetracked by interjections from Hilary. This is another way in which she delayed any responses she may have had.*
Option 2: *This option is correct. Hilary used words like "Right," "OK," and "Uh-huh" to show she was listening. These responses don't mean that she agrees; they just show that she's paying attention and following what Sam is saying.*
Option 3: *This option is incorrect. Hilary remained focused on what Sam was saying. She may*
want to consider the source – Sam – if she chooses to review the feedback more thoroughly afterwards.
Option 4: *This option is incorrect. Hilary did have some negative thoughts, but once she realized what she was doing, she stopped to concentrate on Sam's feedback. When receiving feedback, avoid thinking about how you will respond when it's your turn to speak.*

Once the person is done speaking, you can ask for clarification on anything you don't fully understand. This is step two in the process for receiving feedback. You can also restate what you heard. While this may seem redundant, it can bring to light things you misunderstood that must be clarified.

"Do you mean...?" is an example of a simple way to verify your understanding. You can get clarification by asking for an example to illustrate a point or by providing one of your own. Or you could simply ask the person to be more specific.

The one thing you should avoid is explaining or justifying your actions or behavior. Doing so may sidetrack the feedback and complicate the message.

Sam is finished giving feedback to Hilary. And she's glad she let Sam finish without interrupting because now that she's heard everything he had to say, she's not upset. But she does have a question. Follow along as Hilary seeks clarification.

Hilary: Sam, when you say I should use landmarks as geographical anchors, do you want me to add the actual, existing buildings and fixtures to the model?

Sam: Yes, show prominent, existing landmarks, but also add the things that will be part of the landscape we've designed to complement the facility.

Hilary: OK, so I'll add both existing and proposed landmarks.

Sam: That's right. Homeowners in the area expressed concern that the facility will be an eyesore. I think these changes will really help the stakeholders appreciate how well the design of the facility helps it blend into the existing neighborhood.

Hilary avoided making excuses and moved the discussion forward by asking a question to clarify something she didn't quite understand.

After asking her question, Hilary again listened without interruption to what Sam had to say. She then verified her understanding, which was a good move because it helped her make sure they were both on the same page. Sam agreed and then provided more of an explanation for why the changes are necessary. This series of listening and asking questions demonstrates the iterative nature of feedback.

Now, complete the process of receiving feedback by acknowledging it. If the feedback was truly constructive, you'll likely appreciate it, be thankful for it, and apply it. And your response to the feedback will reflect this.

Hilary listened while Sam delivered his feedback and then the two took turns listening and asking questions as they clarified what needed to be done. Satisfied that they're on the same page, Hilary now wants to acknowledge the feedback. Follow along as Hilary acknowledges Sam's feedback.

Hilary: Thanks for your insight, Sam. I'm now clear on how these changes will improve the presentation.

Sam: Oh, you're welcome, Hilary. That's what teamwork is all about!

What should you do if you **don't** agree with the feedback? You should still remain respectful, but be more neutral. This way you're acknowledging the feedback but not committing to anything.

It may be more important to keep an open mind when you don't agree with feedback. Reconsider what was said and carefully examine whether there's some truth in it. Sometimes when the criticism seems harsh or unjustified, it's hard to find even some valid points you could take to heart.

Because Hilary appreciated and agreed with Sam's feedback, she was able to offer acknowledgement that expressed her willingness to make the changes.

Question

As a member of a team, you need to be able to receive feedback graciously.

Match each element of the process for receiving feedback to the example that best represents it. Not all examples will receive a match.

Options:
A. Listening

B. Clarifying

C. Acknowledging

Targets:

1. "Right."

2. "You want me to use the old process until further notice, is that right?"

3. "I'm so glad you brought this to my attention. I'll try that approach in the future." 4. "Really?"

5. "Now that you got that off your chest, are you ready to get back to work?"

6. "Is there anything you want to clarify further?"

Answer

This is an example of listening. Using receptive language signals you're listening without interjecting.

This is an example of clarifying. This statement directly and assertively communicates your understanding.

This is an example of acknowledging. This statement shows respect, appreciation, and gratitude for the feedback received.

This is not an example of one of the elements. Saying "Really?" while you're supposed to be listening may interrupt the feedback as the person stops to find out what you're questioning.

This is not an example of any of the elements. This could be perceived as dismissive. You need to acknowledge the feedback respectfully, even if you don't agree with it.

This is not an example of any of the elements. If you require clarification or verification, be specific.

Summary

When you're on the receiving end of feedback, you need to be able to take it graciously and in a manner that encourages it.

The process for effectively and graciously receiving feedback is based on three elements: listening without interrupting; clarifying, if necessary; and acknowledging.

Remember to always keep an open mind and be respectful when receiving feedback.

PRACTICE RECEIVING FEEDBACK FROM OTHER TEAM MEMBERS

Receiving feedback

Like giving feedback, receiving feedback becomes easier with practice. Using the elements of the process for receiving feedback – listening, clarifying, and acknowledging – will help to make sure you're gracious and receptive.

Remember, the listening and clarifying elements are iterative. So it's likely you'll find yourself listening and clarifying throughout the process of receiving feedback. And the third element, acknowledging the feedback, is done when both parties agree that they've understood each other.

Now, you can practice what you've learned using the exercise provided. Use each element, as appropriate, to apply your knowledge of the process for receiving feedback.

Case Study: Question 1 of 3

Scenario

For your convenience, the case study is repeated with each question.
Noah has just joined an established team and has noticed that one of its members, Antonio, has a very negative attitude. After attending several meetings where a project wasn't moving forward because Antonio continually displayed a negative atti-

tude, Noah decides it's time to speak with him. Noah has asked Antonio to join him in his office. He wants to tell Antonio how his attitude is impacting the team.

Help Antonio receive this feedback graciously by answering the questions, in order. Question

Noah begins his feedback. "Antonio, I noticed in our meeting today that as you spoke, the mood in the room changed. Once, in reply to Nancy, you said 'How will that be any different from what we did last time? That didn't work either.' Your negativity squashed the team's enthusiasm for finding a solution."

How should Antonio respond?

Options:
1. "Uh-huh."
2. "Oh, really!"
3. "I don't usually do that." 4. "I take offense to that!"
Answer

Option 1: This option is correct. This is hard feedback to take. But, at this point, Antonio needs to be open-minded. Signaling that he's listening as Noah talks is all he should do at this point. Antonio also kept his remark neutral so as to not interrupt the feedback.

Option 2: This option is incorrect. Even though this may be very hard feedback to take, Antonio shouldn't interject with comments that could interrupt the feedback. Only receptive language like "I see" and "Uh-huh" should be used as feedback is given.

Option 3: This option is incorrect. Antonio shouldn't interject while Noah is delivering his feedback. And he really shouldn't be making excuses, which isn't an appropriate response to feedback. Antonio should try to keep an open mind and delay any responses until Noah is finished.

Option 4: This option is incorrect. Antonio shouldn't burst out with a reaction while Noah is delivering feedback. Although this may be hard feedback to take, Antonio should listen without interrupting, and keep an open mind.

Case Study: Question 2 of 3
Scenario

EFFECTIVE TEAMWORK

For your convenience, the case study is repeated with each question.
Noah has just joined an established team and has noticed that one of its members, Antonio, has a very negative attitude. After attending several meetings where a project wasn't moving forward because Antonio continually displayed a negative attitude, Noah decides it's time to speak with him. Noah has asked Antonio to join him in his office. He wants to tell Antonio how his attitude is impacting the team.
Help Antonio receive this feedback graciously by answering the questions, in order. Question
Noah continues with his feedback. "Antonio, maybe you don't even realize you're being so negative. I would like you to try and be more conscious of your remarks. Just pause before you speak to make sure your contributions will move the team forward." What should Antonio say next?

Options:
1. "Do you really think my comments negatively impact the team's productivity?"
2. "I think you should worry about your own impact. The team doesn't take well to new people. I know from experience."
3. "I only said those things because the team never listens to me anyway."
4. "OK, if it will get you to stop criticizing me."

Answer

Option 1: *This option is correct. Antonio waited until Noah finished to verify his understanding of the feedback.*
Option 2: *This option is incorrect. Antonio has deflected the attention back to Noah, but he should remain focused on the feedback. If he has questions, now is the time to ask them.*
Option 3: *This option is incorrect. While this might be true, now isn't the time for Antonio to make excuses for his behavior. No matter why he acted as he did, Antonio needs to accept responsibility for it and move forward.*
Option 4: *This option is incorrect. Antonio should remain open and respectful, not reply defensively. He should take the time to reflect on*

this feedback and search for the truth in it. This is especially true when the feedback is hard to take.

Case Study: Question 3 of 3
Scenario
For your convenience, the case study is repeated with each question.
Noah has just joined an established team and has noticed that one of its members, Antonio, has a very negative attitude. After attending several meetings where a project wasn't moving forward because Antonio continually displayed a negative attitude, Noah decides it's time to speak with him. Noah has asked Antonio to join him in his office. He wants to tell Antonio how his attitude is impacting the team.

Help Antonio receive this feedback graciously by answering the questions, in order. Question

Noah concludes his feedback. "Antonio, your influence is quite strong. That's why I think that if you could direct your contributions in a more positive way, the entire team would benefit. Will you try to be more positive?"

Which response is the most appropriate for Antonio to make now?

Options:
1. "Well, this was hard to hear, but I'll think about what you've said."
2. "Is that all you have to say? I have a deadline I have to meet."
3. "I'll try to be more positive when the team gives me the respect I deserve." 4. "I suppose I could try, but I'm not going to make any promises."

Answer

Option 1: This option is correct. Antonio's language is neutral, but he's respectfully
acknowledging the feedback. This is understandable given the feedback's personal nature.

Option 2: This option is incorrect. This reply is disrespectful and dismissive. Antonio should acknowledge the feedback respectfully, whether he agrees with it or not.

Option 3: *This option is incorrect. This response doesn't focus on the feedback. Antonio has shifted the focus off of himself and onto the team. This attitude won't bring about any positive change.*

Option 4: *This option is incorrect. While Antonio has responded to Noah's request, his response suggests that he isn't trying to find any validity in what Noah has said.*

Summary

As a member of a team, it's your responsibility to develop the interpersonal skills necessary to receive feedback graciously.

Following a simple process for receiving feedback can help: listen without interrupting; clarify, if necessary; and acknowledge the feedback.

Like all of your team interactions, be respectful and keep an open mind, and receiving feedback will be the productive, performance-improving activity it's meant to be.

www.ingramcontent.com/pod-product-compliance
Lightning Source LLC
Chambersburg PA
CBHW060842220526
45466CB00003B/1211